THE
DECENTERED
UNIVERSE
OF
FINNEGANS WAKE

A Structuralist Analysis

MARGOT NORRIS

THE JOHNS HOPKINS UNIVERSITY PRESS
Baltimore and London

To my grandmother,
Leopoldine Hochberger

This book has been brought to publication with the generous assistance of the Andrew W. Mellon Foundation.

Manufactured in the United States of America

The Johns Hopkins University Press, Baltimore, Maryland 21218
The Johns Hopkins Press Ltd., London

Library of Congress Catalog Card Number 76–25507
ISBN 0–8018–1820–6

Library of Congress Cataloging in Publication data will be found on the last printed page of this book.

CONTENTS

ACKNOWLEDGMENTS

A first book is always a collaborative effort. Mine has in it much of the teaching, dialogue, and example of my instructors. Joseph Riddel's lectures on structuralism provided me with those large and subtle ideas in the modern tradition that make a whole new approach to literature possible and that gave me the confidence to try to shed some light on *Finnegans Wake*. His counsel played the most vital part in generating the theoretical framework of the book. One of my biggest challenges was the effort to write lucidly, about a very opaque work, in the difficult language of the structuralist method. Mark Shechner deserves credit for helping some stylistic clarity survive this challenge, and for augmenting my lean theories with his own sensitive readings of Joyce and Freud. Albert Cook's astute suggestions informed the major revisions of the original dissertation. All of this professional help was given with much generosity, and with a friendship that continues to sustain me in my academic life.

Portions of this book have previously appeared as articles in journals: "The Consequence of Deconstruction: A Technical Perspective of Joyce's *Finnegans Wake*," in *ELH, A Journal of English Literary History*, vol. 41, no. 1, Spring 1974, published by The Johns Hopkins University Press; "The Function of Mythic Repetition in *Finnegans Wake*," in *James Joyce Quarterly*, vol. 11, no. 4, Summer 1974, published by the University of Tulsa; "The Language of Dream in

Finnegans Wake," in *Literature and Psychology,* vol. 24, no. 1, 1974. I wish to thank these journals for their permission to use this material here.

Manly Johnson, Charmaine Wellington, and Betty Stokes helped with the final preparation of the manuscript. I am grateful to the University of Tulsa for helping to underwrite the publication costs of this work.

There are others, always, whose influence on a work like this is indirect, but whose affection and faith are necessary ingredients: my family, particularly my uncle, Ernst Hochberger; my favorite professor at the University of Florida, T. Walter Herbert; my feminist sisters in Buffalo and Tulsa; Christopher D. Morris; and my eleven-year-old son, Josef, whose liberated views on working mothers make many things possible.

ABBREVIATIONS

The primary texts used in this work are all American editions of Joyce's work. The following abbreviations are adopted:

CM *Chamber Music.* New York: The Viking Press, 1972.

D   *Dubliners.* New York: The Viking Press, 1962.

F   *Finnegans Wake.* New York: The Viking Press, 1971.

P   *A Portrait of the Artist as a Young Man.* New York: The Viking Press, 1975.

U   *Ulysses.* New York: Random House, 1966.

Book/chapter and page/line numbers for *Finnegans Wake* are included in parentheses in the text without a preceding symbol. Book/chapter numbers are given as follows: I. 3 (Book I, Chapter 3). Page/line references indicate the line on which the quotation begins and are given as follows: 338.9 (page 338, line 9). Footnotes in *Finnegans Wake* are indicated in the following manner: F4 (footnote 4).

INTRODUCTION

THE CRITICAL METHOD

STRUCTURE AND LANGUAGE

Thanks to the patient toil of its dedicated explicators, the major contours of Joyce's *Finnegans Wake* have gradually come into focus in the thirty-five years since its publication. Yet while more allusions, motifs, and linguistic details are continually coming to light, the intellectual orientation of the work remains largely obscure.

The attempt to assess the teleology of *Finnegans Wake* has always presented critics with a dilemma: the choice between a radical and a conservative interpretation of the book. A radical interpretation would maintain that *Finnegans Wake* subverts not only the literary status quo but the most cherished intellectual preconceptions of Western culture as well—a position most clearly maintained in the pioneer studies of the work. Yet in these early studies, such as *Our Exagmination,*[1] the weakness of the radical interpretation also becomes apparent. While proclaiming the revolutionary nature of *Work in Progress,* the writers lack scholarly pegs on which to hang their theories and finally resort to ad hoc analogies to support their theses. In contrast, the conservative critics, who have dominated *Wake* criticism for the last thirty years, possess a small but scholarly arsenal: the stylistic and thematic conservatism of the early manuscript drafts, the inclusion of traditional, even arcane, literary material in the work, Joyce's admission that the work's structural and philosophical models are derived from a six-teenth-century metaphysician and an eighteenth-century philosopher, and finally, Joyce's own decidedly reactionary tastes. Even the recently published *A Conceptual Guide to "Finnegans Wake,"*[2] which aims at a comprehensive study of the work, embraces this conservative tradition by approaching the work as a novel: "along with the problem for the reader of deciphering Joyce's language goes the stumbling block of figuring out the narrative or the plot."

Joyce is himself partly responsible for this unsettled state of affairs. Throughout the progress of his writing, he sent friends and disciples scurrying to reference books that would unlock the secret of a phrase or passage, while his comments on the overall purpose and construction of the book remained enigmatic and vague—often phrased in negative terms that suggest what *Finnegans Wake* is not, rather than what it is. "I might easily have written this story in the traditional manner. . . . Every novelist knows the recipe. . . . It is not very difficult to follow a simple, chronological scheme which the critics will understand. . . . But I, after all, am trying to tell the story of this Chapelizod family in a new way. . . . "[3] We are left to wonder about the nature of this new way of telling the story. Joyce's sanction and supervision of *Our Exagmination* was clearly an effort to answer this question. Yet while approving his disciples' defense of his work on radical grounds, he failed to supply them with a theoretical base other than his references to Bruno and Vico.

Since the time of these pioneer *Wake* critics, an enormous amount of detailed explication of the text has become available, and new tools for critical investigation have emerged that make it possible to examine more thoroughly those aspects of the work that resist novelistic analysis. With these advantages, I hope to resume the radical viewpoints of the early critics and demonstrate the extent of the challenge that Joyce offered not only to conventional literary modes but also to many of the epistemological presuppositions of our culture. My argument will be based on the assumption that Joyce did not mount this challenge in a vacuum, but that knowingly or unknowingly he participated in those intellectual currents of early-twentieth-century Europe, whose destructive impact depended on a profound revision of the understanding of language. Eugene Jolas, a close personal friend and colleague of Joyce's, was extraordinarily sensitive to these currents. "The real metaphysical problem today is the word," he writes in *Our Exagmination*. "The new artist of the word has recognized the autonomy of language."[4] Jolas also connected Joyce with the literary experimentalists of the day.

> Léon-Paul Fargue, one of the great French poets of our age, has created astonishing neologisms in his prose poems. . . . The revolution of the surrealists, who destroyed completely the old relationships between words and thought, remains of immense significance. . . . André Breton, demoralizing the old psychic processes by the destruction of logic, has discovered a world of magic in the study of dream via the Freudian explorations. . . . Miss Gertrude Stein attempts to find a mysticism of the word by the process of thought thinking itself.[5]

At the time Jolas proclaimed "the revolution of the word," modern theoretical linguistics was in its infancy.[6] Ferdinand de Saussure's *Course in General Linguistics* was published in Paris in 1910 but appears to have gone unnoticed by contemporary writers. And yet we find in *Finnegans Wake* that intellectual shift which locates meaning in relationships and structure rather than in content—a shift formalized by Saussure's recognition of the arbitrary nature of the linguistic sign and his focus on the synchronic laws of language.

Among the many shocks administered to the Victorian mentality during the early twentieth century, the power and scope of the unconscious in human life was perhaps the least sensational but the most enduring. Freud's discovery of the extent to which man's psychic and emotional life is controlled by his unconscious adumbrated the complex role that language plays in that process. Psychoanalyst Jacques Lacan has recently restored this aspect of Freud's theory to prominence.[7] But those marvelously complicated workings of the unconscious that give us language were not truly recognized until Noam Chomsky's devastating refutation of behaviorist linguistic theory in the 1950s. Further evidence of man's lack of self-knowledge and impaired understanding of his condition ultimately served to raise criticism to the status of a highly self-conscious, creative act. In recent times this brand of self-reflexive criticism has expanded to many disciplines in a movement known broadly as structuralism. The theoretical roots of the structuralist method lie in linguistics, but its application ranges across the diverse human sciences, with particularly interesting developments in anthropology, psychoanalysis, and philosophy.

Structuralism presupposes that the organization of psychic and social life is based on similar unconscious laws and that the structures that underlie various human activities—language, family relationships, religious worship, social communications, for example—are therefore isomorphic. Consequently, relationships rather than substances, structures rather than contents, provide significant sources of meaning in human institutions and systems of communication.

Structuralist theory is stubbornly at variance with those prevailing political and social philosophies that exhibit a distinct behaviorist bias, an underlying faith that man is shaped by the external forces of his environment and that human betterment depends on the improvement of that environment. Yet it is precisely this conflict that helps to illustrate the suitability of the structuralist approach to Joyce's work. In their grim depiction of the spiritual "paralysis" that Dublin visits on its citizens, *Dubliners* and *A Portrait of the Artist as a Young Man* (hereafter cited as *Portrait*) affirm the oppression of the individual by society and its institutions. But while Joyce is unconcerned with melioration in these works, his theme of exile does promise hope of escape. The local use of mythic patterns in *Portrait* expands in *Ulysses* to a massive mythic structure that ascribes the condition of the individual not merely to accidents of environment but to certain constant predispositions in his own nature and in the order of things as well. For example, the "brutal" fathers in *Dubliners,* Farrington and Little Chandler, are so crushed by their environments that they take their anger and frustration out on their small sons. But father-son relationships in *Ulysses* have become symbolic and complex. Stephen's *Hamlet* theory and numerous mythic analogues isolate recurrent difficulties that plague the hierarchical systems in which men relate to each other and to their gods. In *Finnegans Wake* the notion of an "environment"— which depends on an empirical belief in the separation of inner and outer, subjective and objective, mental and physical—completely disintegrates. Characters are fluid and interchangeable, melting easily into their landscapes to become river and land, tree and stone, Howth Castle and Environs, or HCE. We find in the *Wake* not characters as such but ciphers, in formal relationship to each other.

For all his reticence on the subject, Joyce did provide a single helpful clue to orient our approach to his new universe. Preceded by a theory of correspondences that he derived from Hermes Trismegistus and Swedenborg (cf. *P*, p. 244), his last work employed the thought of Giordano Bruno, which he summarized as follows: "His philosophy is a kind of dualism—every power in nature must evolve an opposite in order to realise itself and opposition brings reunion etc etc."[8] Besides its resemblance to Hegelian dialectic, Bruno's philosophical dualism adumbrates the binary opposition of phonemes, which provided a central insight into the nature of linguistic meaning: meaning inheres not in sounds themselves—"d" and "t," for example—but in the contrast or difference between them, so that we can distinguish "dime" and "time." The concept of binary opposition is a cornerstone of the structuralist method. "But when, as in structuralism, substance is replaced by relationship, then the noun, the object, even the individual ego itself, becomes nothing but a locus of cross-references: not things, but differential perceptions, that is to say, a sense of the *identity* of a given element which derives solely from our awareness of its *difference* from other elements, and ultimately from an implicit comparison of it with its own opposite."[9] I will try to use this method in a central, integrated approach to the entire work, its narrative structure, its themes, the nature of the discourse (point of view), and the technical and aesthetic aspects of the language.

DREAM THEORY

For all its stylistic innovations, *Ulysses* ceased to bedazzle critics and readers and started to "make sense" once the plot and story line were discovered and understood. Similar attempts to transcend the pyrotechnics of *Finnegans Wake* have more or less failed. Story lines and plots have had to be plugged with hallucinations and dreams within dreams. Yet annoying questions concerning the nature of the figures, events, and language have persisted all the same. I have tried to approach *Finnegans Wake* with an abiding trust in Joyce's artistry and professional experience and a modicum of trust in my own good sense as a reader and critic. I have resisted the promptings of armchair psychology to chalk up the puzzling and confusing nature of the work to Joyce's mischief, malice, or megalomania. And after much study, thought, and irritation, I have come to the conclusion that the key to the puzzle is the puzzle. In other words, expecting the work to "make sense" in the way *Portrait, Ulysses,* or traditional novels "make sense" implies a conceptual framework and epistemology that Joyce strongly intimated he wanted to undermine. *Finnegans Wake* is a puzzle because dreams are puzzles—elaborate, brilliant, purposeful puzzles, which constitute a universe quite unlike any we know or experience in waking life.

Although Freud's influence on Joyce is argued convincingly by

Frederick J. Hoffman in his early essay[10] and endorsed by Atherton,[11] Clive Hart's preference for the *Upanishads* as the source of Joyce's dream theory[12] makes some restatement necessary. Joyce's reference to Freud's *The Interpretation of Dreams* in *Finnegans Wake* (338.29) is supported by ample evidence that he read the book with care and applied the techniques of dream-work to the *Wake*. Virtually every one of the "typical dreams" described by Freud[13] constitutes a major theme in *Finnegans Wake*. "Embarrassing Dreams of Being Naked," which often find the subject naked before strangers, are reflected in the voyeurism of the three anonymous soldiers in the Phoenix Park incident. Freud points out that frequently the strangers in such dreams represent familiar persons: the *Wake*'s soldiers represent HCE's sons, who view their father much as the sons of Noah viewed their father. Explaining dreams about the death of beloved persons, Freud discusses both sibling rivalry and the simultaneous incestuous and murderous feelings between parents and children. All of these taboos are at issue in the mysterious sin in *Finnegans Wake*. In fact, Freud reports a dream that contains a cluster of the elements found in the Phoenix Park incident. It shows "two boys struggling," like the *Wake*'s enemy twins, with one of them fleeing for protection to a maternal woman, like ALP hiding the "lipoleums" under her skirt hoop to "sheltershock" (8.30) them. Freud interprets the woman as representing both an incestuous and a voyeuristic object for the boy. "The dream combined two opportunities he had had as a little boy of seeing little girls' genitals: When they were *thrown down* and when they were *micturating.* And from the other part of the context it emerged that he had a recollection of being *chastised* or threatened by his father for the sexual curiosity he had evinced on these occasions."[14] Freud's dream resembles the homework chapter, II.2, where the boys examine their mother's genitals and one boy strikes the other in punishment. The merging of the boy with the threatening father in Freud's dream also recurs frequently in a merger of father and son in the *Wake*. Furthermore, the notion of voyeuristically watching girls urinate is a repeated Phoenix Park/Waterloo image. Freud discusses both children's games and examinations or academic tests as bearing sexual significance in typical dreams, a concept manifested in Chapters II.1 and II.2 of *Finnegans Wake*.

The dream universe is structured differently from the mental universe of conscious life because meanings are located in different places. One explanation for the encyclopedic nature of *Finnegans Wake* is that the dreaming psyche attaches items of knowledge or information from the waking consciousness and invests them with totally different meanings. The key to the new meanings is hidden in the connection between the two thoughts. For example, "Waterloo" means a famous Napoleonic battle to the waking mind. In the Wakean dream world it also means a place for urinating. If "Waterloo" reminds the dreamer of a juvenile chastisement for watching girls urinate, then the sexual and historical references to the place become linked by the common theme of humiliating defeat. Because meanings are dislocated—hidden in unexpected places, multiplied and split, given over to ambiguity, plurality, and uncertainty—the dream represents a decentered universe. Since this dream universe is so unlike waking life, the critical techniques designed to explore the traditional novel are unsuitable to the study of a dream-work. To examine various aspects of this decentered world, I have borrowed the ideas and tools of theoreticians in a variety of fields who share an interest in the structures of the systems they study.

The narrative structure of *Finnegans Wake,* which I discuss in Chapter 2, appears more intelligible in the light of the modern myth theories of anthropologist Claude Lévi-Strauss than it did through attempts at finding correspondences to the Gilbert scheme for *Ulysses.* Lévi-Strauss's myth theory suggests a plausible reason for Joyce's "new way" of telling a story by collocating versions of the same event rather than developing a chronological plot. Furthermore, Lévi-Strauss's concept of the homology of myth and dream suggests a way of relating individual and social experience in *Finnegans Wake* without recourse to the Jungian concept of a "collective unconscious." While Lévi-Strauss argues that myths and dreams are governed by the same unconscious structures and that the meaning of myths and dreams resides in the relationships between their elements, Jungian theory posits the significance and persistence of the nature of types and images in the personal and racial memory.

The relationships between Wakean figures have such complex functions that a series of interlocking approaches was required in Chapter 3 to describe them adequately. Insofar as these relationships are power relationships, they constitute a destructive and repetitive system that is reflected in the theories of Vico, Freud, and Hegel. Vico's socioreligious history is based on endless cycles produced by mankind's progress from one age to another as power relationships change. The sexual dynamic of the Freudian family is based on unconscious power relationships that were operative in establishing primitive society. The power relationships implicit in Hegel's Master-slave dialectic relate the concept of the fight to the emergence of human consciousness—a notion elaborated on at the psychoanalytic level by Jacques Lacan. The paradoxical nature of society as simultaneously lawful and repressive is reversed by the anarchic Oedipal drives in the *Wake*, which create a decentered dream world that is without law, but free.

The dream permits the dreamer's relationship to himself to assume dramatic form as he uses the disguises and defenses provided by the dream mechanism to communicate to himself about himself. Philosopher Martin Heidegger's theory of inauthentic being helps to explore the ontological condition of the dreamer through his comportment toward guilt, truth, and death.

Chapter 5 explores dream language as poetic language, using Lacan's theories of language, repression, and poetry. It is the function of a dream to simultaneously conceal and reveal the nature of the "true" or unconscious self, a task accomplished through the structural operations described by Freud. Such techniques of dream-work as displacement, condensation, and distortion, correspond to the tropes that create the dense, ambiguous, polyvalent language of the work. The tension in the language, which bars semantic certainty or simplicity, signifies the decentered universe it expresses.

My final chapter treats the philosophical implications of expressing a decentered universe—a problem formulated by philosopher Jacques Derrida as a critical dilemma. In Joyce's case, the problem is technical—the need to find a language to depict a world in which identities are unstable, speakers are deceptive and lack self-knowledge, the point of view is not unified, and the society depicted is anarchic.

Throughout this discussion I have spoken of a dreamer and of the dream of *Finnegans Wake* as though there is indeed a single dreamer and I know exactly who he is. Well, I don't know who he is. To say that Joyce is the dreamer tells us nothing useful. To say that the dreamer is Finn or Earwicker ignores the significance of ambiguous identities in the dream. Wakean figures are interchangeable because characters in dreams are fictions created by the dreamer—including fictions of himself. In other words, the dreamer is invested in all of his characters in certain ways, and the characters that represent himself are no less fictional than any of the others. I suspect that we are to assume a single dreamer, since the same obsessions inform all the themes narrated by the different voices. The different speaking voices may therefore represent different personae of the dreamer relating different versions of the same event. For example, since a single dreamer can be a father, a son, and a brother all at once, he can play out an Oedipal drama in his dream, in which he takes the parts of Laius, Oedipus, and Creon all at once. In this way he can express many conflicting feelings simultaneously. I speculate that it makes no difference whether one supposes a single long dream, with constant repetition of the same theme, or a group of serial dreams, each dealing with the same theme. It seems plausible to suppose that the dreamer is male, since the major conflicts appear to afflict male figures. But sex, like everything else, is mutable in dreams. The question "Who is the dreamer?" is a question properly addressed not to the reader but to the dreamer himself, who discovers in the dream that he is by no means who he thinks he is.

1

READING
FINNEGANS
WAKE

THE NOVELISTIC FALLACY

In an early essay, Harry Levin wrote of *Finnegans Wake:*

Concretely, there are at least three misconceptions that threaten to shape our total impression of *Finnegans Wake.* The first of these is that, while not differing greatly in kind from the books we are accustomed to read, it happens to have been written in a rather queer language, and must therefore undergo the process of translation to which all foreign books—including the Scandinavian—are regularly subjected. . . . A second, and related, fallacy is that *Finnegans Wake* is a novel. Herein is the real reason for putting critical emphasis on the 'story' and brusquely attempting to extract a quintessential content from the morass of form in which it lies embedded.[1]

The persistence and authority of the novelistic assumption in criticisms of *Finnegans Wake* have been greater than even Harry Levin could have foreseen. Before launching a study of the *Wake* as a dream-work, it might be helpful to probe the "novelistic fallacy" by examining *Finnegans Wake* in the light of the fundamental presuppositions and characteristics of the traditional novel.

Ian Watt in *The Rise of the Novel* (Berkeley: University of California Press, 1967) locates the philosophical roots of the novel in the subjectivism of eighteenth-century thought. He cites specifically the belief in the individual's claim to knowledge and truth through his senses, independent from the collective tradition of the past, as the cornerstone of realist epistemology. This view is manifested in the novelistic plot, which portrays the individual's experience as the testing ground of reality and thereby justifies the exploration of everyday life in literature.

Finnegans Wake fails to support these novelistic premises and, indeed, there is ample evidence to suggest that the work is designed precisely to refute the realist epistemology that has dominated prose fiction since the eighteenth century. The narrative technique of *Finnegans Wake* challenges the primacy of subjective individual experience in several ways. The singularity of individual experience—its uniqueness—is undermined by the replication of events and the instability of characters. The causal relationship of events in novelistic narration is replaced in *Finnegans Wake* by contiguous associations on the order of psychoanalytic free associations. Watt also points out that the novel requires a language that is concerned less with rhetorical beauty than with the correspondence of words to things. The novel, in fact, fairly takes this correspondence for granted. *Finnegans Wake,* in contrast, self-reflexively insists on the mediation of events by language; all events in the *Wake* are merely stories, and it is impossible to determine whether they represent history or fiction.

This antisubjectivism implicit in the narrative structure of the work is most easily illustrated by comparing a theme common to both Joyce's own novelistic *Portrait* and *Finnegans Wake.* Although myth and history have revealed that fathers and sons are locked primordially and inevitably into a struggle for supremacy, Stephen Dedalus in *Portrait* comes to an awareness of this conflict through a concrete, personal experience: his trip to Cork with his father. The decline of Simon Dedalus's financial fortunes requires the sale of his Cork property at auction. The miserable condition of his return to the scenes of his youth prompts in the old man nostalgia, self-pity, fear, and defensiveness in the face of his impending decline and fall.

By God, I don't feel more than eighteen myself. There's that son of mine there not half my age and I'm a better man than he is any day of the week.

    —Draw it mild now, Dedalus. I think it's time for you to take a back seat, said the gentleman who had spoken before.

    —No, by God! asserted Mr. Dedalus. I'll sing a tenor song against him or I'll vault a fivebarred gate against him or I'll run with him after the hounds across the country as I did thirty years ago along with the Kerry Boy and the best man for it.

—But he'll beat you here, said the little old man, tapping his forehead and raising his glass to drain it. (*P*, p. 95)

Stephen learns of his mythic struggle with his father through his senses and his consciousness—by listening to the tavern banter of the old men, by noting his father's displeasure at the little old man's hints that he relinquish his post to his son. In *Ulysses* Stephen responds to the little old man, as it were, by repeating the brow-tapping gesture and then formalizing his filial aggression in the impersonal terms of symbolic confrontation—"(*He taps his brow.*) But in here it is I must kill the priest and the king." (*U*, p. 589) In the dream world of *Finnegans Wake,* the father's fear of the son's ascendance is never vested in a unique experience, like the visit to the Cork tavern, or in direct expression, like Simon Dedalus's acknowledged anxiety over his perilous physical brawn. Only the psychological reality of the father's fear is expressed, which in the unguarded arena of dream takes monstrous shape in images of military defeat and sexual humiliation by the sons—far beyond anything old Dedalus might dare confess to himself.

In *Portrait,* the motive for the father-son tension seems to reside in the individuals themselves, in the pride of both father and son and their bitter humiliation in recognizing the failings of the father. The moment in the Cork pub takes its significance from the entire preceding family history: the erstwhile prosperity of the rich, powerful father, and his subsequent financial and personal decline ending in bankruptcy, drunkenness, and self-contempt. In *Finnegans Wake,* the father-son tensions arise not from the particular psychic constitutions of individuals but from the nature of the relationship itself. In other words, father-son conflict resides in the order of things, in the unconscious law that governs social life and decrees that society's continuation demands replacement of fathers by sons. In *Finnegans Wake,* the warning to the father of the son's ascendance is therefore not vested in the exigency of the specific historical moment but, rather, in a series of involuntary fantasies and images.

28.35 there's already a big rody ram lad at random on the premises of his haunt of the hungred bordles, as it is told me.

383.9 *You're the rummest old rooster ever flopped out of a Noah's ark*
And you think you're cock of the wark.
Fowls, up! Tristy's the spry young spark

452.29 We only wish everyone was as sure of anything in this watery world as we are of everything in the newlywet fellow that's bound to follow.

607.14   It is their segnall for old Champelysied to seek the shades of his retirement and for young Chappielassies to tear a round and tease their partners lovesoftfun at Finnegan's Wake.

627.6   I pity your oldself I was used to. Now a younger's there.

The movement of the father's decline and fall in *Portrait* is logical and linear, from high to low. The prosperous gentleman who carves the turkey at the sumptuous Christmas feast later presides with a harsh whistle over a dirty household of slovenly tea, broken clocks, and lousy children. The father's fall is caused by excesses, particularly drink, and *Portrait* focuses on the son's blame of the father. *Finnegans Wake,* however, explores the father's guilt for his sins, which include not only drink, like Simon Dedalus's, but also incestuous and other perverse sexual desires, like Leopold Bloom's. Furthermore, the chronology of the father's fall is reversed, so that his guilt breeds the imagined accusations that generate investigations into his sins. This reversal is appropriate to the dream, in which the systems of cause and effect governing actions in the waking world no longer apply. Since the traditional novel simulates the logic of waking life, its conventions are not to be found in the Wakean dream world, in which desires, fantasies, and fears enjoy the status of actions, and fictions are accorded the status of facts. Finally, the sins of the father are irrelevant to his fall in *Finnegans Wake,* because the fall is a social inevitability, a result of unconscious laws, or "the rules of sport," as the rann declares.

For be all rules of sport 'tis right
That youth bedower'd to charm the night
Whilst age is dumped to mind the day
When wather parted from the say. (371.18) (my alignment)

The unconscious connects contiguous thoughts by free association into labyrinthian sequences. Even in early sections of *Ulysses,* Joyce structures conversations on the principle of free association. One of Stephen's first conversations with Mulligan meanders along an improbable course from a request for a handkerchief to the death of Stephen's mother by way of the common color of snot, sea, and bile. In the dream world of *Finnegans Wake,* narrative cohesion is achieved by contiguity on an even larger scale. A typical Wakean sentence serves to illustrate how contiguous associations create a vertical depth along a narrative line.

It was of The Grant, old gartener, *qua* golden meddlist, Publius Manlius, fuderal private, (his place is his poster, sure, they said, and we're going to mark it, sore, they said, with a carbon caustick manner) bequother the liberaloider at his petty corporelezzo that hung caughtnapping from his baited breath, it was of him, my wife and I thinks, to feel to every of the younging fruits, tenderosed like an atalantic's breastswells or, on a second wreathing, a bright tauth bight shimmery-shaking for the welt of his plow. (336.21)

This sentence entwines at least four major myths or tales, whose common factor is the theme of the fall: the *Wake* story of Buckley's shooting of the Russian General, the biblical myth of Adam's fall, the Greek myth of the race of Atalanta, and the story of the demise of Melville's Billy Budd.

The themes of the Buckley–Russian General story and Billy Budd are linked through the klang-association of Buckley-Budd[2] and by their common military context. Each involves an execution, a shooting on land, and a hanging at sea, respectively. The Crimean war setting of the Buckley–Russian General tale has shifted to the American Civil War, and the HCE figure is now a much-decorated Ulysses S. Grant ("The Grant" . . . "a golden meddlist") as well as a federal, or pro-Union ("fuderal"), private. The old soldier will be devastated by simulta-neously having his poster defaced ("mark") with charcoal ("a carbon caustick") and being shot ("mark") in the rear ("postern": hidden, dishonorable entrance) with a carbine ("carbon") rifle ("caustick"). The Billy Budd references are less obvious, but we find several sugges-tions of hanging ("hung caughtnapping from his baited breath;" "a bright tauth bight," "bight": loop of rope, "tau": T-shaped cross or gallows), and of the sea ("atalantic's breastswells": waves on the shore of the Atlantic; "bight": curve in a bay; "welt," welter: to toss as on water; "plow": to cut a path through the sea). We find also references to two stellar constellations ("wreath": Corona Australis and "plow": Ursa major), which may serve as references to Captain "Starry" Vere in *Billy Budd.*

The Billy Budd tale suits the HCE fall motif perfectly, even though the conflict configuration appears to be precisely reversed— filicidal rather than patricidal. The two are strikingly similar in that Billy Budd's downfall, like HCE's in the cad and tavern confrontations, begins with a malicious accusation that triggers a response of fatal self-defense. Furthermore, Billy's flaw resembles HCE's—"an organic hesitancy, in fact more or less of a stutter,"[3] perhaps the "baited breath" in the *Wake* passage.

In the passage under consideration, Old Testament Adam is referred to as a grand "old gartener," who reaches for the apple ("younging fruits"). His bite ("bight") costs him Eden ("atalantic" refers also to Atlantis, another lost continent) and damns him to till the land by the sweat of his brow ("welt of his plow"). The common element of the biblical Eden myth and the Greek myth of Atalanta is, of course, the apple. Atalanta loses the race because she stoops to pick up the apples ("feel to every of the younging fruits"). The image of the apples merges with images of golden medals ("golden meddlist"). Atalanta's breasts ("tenderosed": tender rose, tenderized, or tenderly arose), and the shimmering curve of the bay ("on a second wreathing, a bright tauth bight shimmeryshaking"). The erotic references to fruits and breasts are clues to HCE's misdeeds.

While widely separated according to chronology and genre, the four fictions represented in the foregoing *Wake* paragraph are compressed through the function of contiguous sounds, images, and themes. The analogue of this phenomenon in Freudian dream-work is, of course, condensation. In those instances of linguistic condensation, such as wreathing (reading), Grant (grand), welt of his plow (sweat of his brow), we see the linguistic departure of *Wake* narrative from traditional novelistic technique. Whereas the novel requires a prose that stresses semantic precision, the correspondence of words to things, the dream technique in *Finnegans Wake* requires words that are semantically polyvalent and whose meanings are deliberately uncertain.

These various departures of *Finnegans Wake* from the traditional novel—replicated events, unstable characters, contiguous associations, semantic vagary—suggest something more than an enrichment of the art form, or even its decadence after a long and fruitful history. Rather, these departures signify a critique of the novel itself and, consequently, a critique of the literary and intellectual traditions that have sustained it.

THE INTEGRATION OF ELEMENTS

A major difficulty with the novelistic approach to *Finnegans Wake* concerns the integration of fabulous and naturalistic elements in the work. By granting primacy to a novelistic story line, one finds it necessary to interpolate the fantastic elements in the work into a linear narrative, perhaps as tales told by the customers in the pub or as dreams within dreams,[4] and the myths, fables, riddles, and stories must be relegated to the function of a superstructure that illustrates, universalizes, and inflates the literal events. In other words, naturalistic and mythic events are regarded as allegorically related—"symbolic" to "real," if you will. This approach leads to analyses of Wakean characters as true-to-life figures—analyses that ignore such insistent issues as the shifting and questionable identities of Wakean figures. Yet James Atherton writes, "There are too many real—or rather, fully realized—characters taking part in the action for the book to be anything except a novel of the naturalistic type."[5]

By contrasting a traditional "content" approach with a "structure" approach, I would like to show how mythic and naturalistic elements can be integrated without the necessity of establishing one or the other as a dominant point of reference.

In a chapter entitled "Growing Up Absurd in Dublin," Hugh Staples finds in the details of Shaun's personality the key to the meaning of Book III. "The Shaun of III.1," he writes, "wants to be thought of as a man-about-town, a snappy dresser, a glutton and a gourmet. He is possessed of a musical voice and he is a braggart. . . . He is not happy in his work, which is that of a messenger or a postman; he would prefer to be a priest."[6] Proposing that younger brother Charlie Joyce is reflected in the composite Shaun portrait of III, he goes on to describe Jaun's preparations for the journey in III.2 as a story of the problems of adolescence: "Jaun's preoccupations are typically adolescent: what career to take up in life. . . . Jaun remains fundamentally incomplete, adolescent and sometimes even infantile in his relationship with women."[7] Staples brushes aside Joyce's own suggestion that the *via crucis* is a structuring device in the chapter: "In my view, elements of such a matrix are at best vestigial, and I think, unimportant. . . . For me, the Christian elements in *Finnegans Wake* remain for the most part decorative, rather than structural."[8] Staples gathers together the details revealed about a character's life style, his actions, his feelings toward others, his ambitions, and arrives at a portrait—the depiction of a novelistic character who is "full," who has content.

Evidence shows, however, that both biblical and liturgical references are dense enough in the three Shaun chapters[9] to suggest that Joyce's hint about a *via crucis* was not merely an idea he later discarded. Remembering Bruno's dictum as well as the contrary nature of the dream, we need not look for a Christ-like figure in Shaun, or events strictly parallel to the passion of Christ, or a *via crucis* ordered precisely like the original.

Jesus carrying his cross, Shaun carrying his letter to save HCE, the ass bearing the Gospel of the four evangelists, or even the politician running in an election race—all are on missions of redemption ("mailman of peace . . . bearer extraordinary of these postoomany missive on his majesty's service" [408.10]). Joyce is here using a dream technique that occurs throughout *Finnegans Wake,* the animation of a pun, in this case "deliverance," meaning both salvation and running an errand. The action may also represent a priest saying Mass, another act of redemption in the form of a reenactment or drama—which may account for the dramatic elements in this chapter. Shaun, dressed like the postman of Boucicault's play,[10] resembles a priest in a coat of "far suparior ruggedness" (404.18) (Father Superior, and a chasublelike garment with "surpliced crinklydoodle front with his motto through dear life embrothred over it . . . R.M.D." [404.28])—dramatically reenacting the redemptive act of Christ. But the would-be savior, stuffed with an enormous Last-Supper-like meal, is too fat and lazy to go on. So he sinks "his hunk, dowanouet to resk at once, exhaust as winded hare" (408.3), and wishes plaintively ("Weh is me, yeh is ye" [408.15]) that his brother might take his place ("It should of been my other" [408.17])—like Jesus praying that the cup may pass from him in Gethsemane. The Mass goes on, and Shaun, as priest complaining of all the kneeling and movement, and as Christ complaining of his burden, whines, "Lard have mustard on them! Fatiguing, very fatiguing. Hobos hornknees and the corveeture of my spine. Poumeerme! My heaviest crux and dairy lot it is" (409.15). The complaints continue: "I am now becoming about fed up be going circulating about them new hikler's highways" (410.7) and "I am hopeless off course" (410.18). Later he explains to those two "pedestriasts" (410.35), the two thieves (410.36), or perhaps two acolytes, how he ought "to be disbarred after holy orders from unnecessary servile work of reckless walking of all sorts" (411.2).

Staples finds in this discussion a mailman, unhappy with his job, who would rather be a priest. Simple reference to the *via crucis,* however, illustrates Bruno's contraries at work and describes Shaun in terms of his opposite. Unlike Christ, praying in bitter anguish to be spared the impending passion, Shaun sniffs in pusillanimous whimpers about the hardship of his route. While Christ falls under the crushing weight of the cross, Shaun sinks to the ground under the crushing weight of his own obesity, having eaten an obscenely huge Last Supper.

Although Tindall gives a helpful summary of the references in III.2 to each of the fourteen Stations of the Cross,[11] it is important to note the inversions here as well. The meetings between Jesus and the various women on his journey to Calvary, his mother, Veronica, and the weeping women (including "Marie Maudlin" [434.16]), are here presented in the form of Jaun's double-talking sermon—sanctimonious and prurient—and Issy's brief reply. Joyce strategically combines events and characters. The mother of Jesus and Veronica merge in the figure of sister Isabel, for whom Jaun harbors incestuous affections ("he was brotherbesides her benedict godfather and heaven knows he thought the world and his life of her sweet heart" [431.18]). The weeping women are also the twenty-nine schoolgirls of St. Bride's. The events of Calvary that involve clothing are also compressed. Jesus being stripped of his garment and Veronica removing and offering her veil are events transformed in the chapter into mutual displays of exhibitionism and voyeurism. The Black Mass motif of sitting naked on the tabernacle ("Tubber Nakel" [438.13]), while bush rangers look on, connects Jesus stripping before the "peeping private" (438.15) to the three voyeuristic soldiers who watch HCE in Phoenix Park.

The "veronique" (458.14) that Isabel presents to Jaun is a last-moment gift, some "memento nosepaper" (457.34). Issy wants him to use it as notepaper, to write to her ("Of course, please too write, won't you" [458.18]), and send it by carrier pigeon (or Holy Ghost, perhaps). It may be just a tissue or paper handkerchief to wipe the bleeding face of Christ, and Issy worries about the sanitation of loaning her version of Stephen's "snotrag" ("That's the stupidest little cough. Only be sure you don't catch your cold and pass it on to us" [458.11]). But Issy may suspect that the illness is terminal, in which case the "memento nosepaper" becomes a newspaper obituary that she wants sent if "any funforall happens I'll be so curiose to see in the Homesworth breakfast tablotts . . . in case I don't hope to soon hear from you" (458.22). There is also a sinister hint that Isabel may be wanting to sell the valuable relic or autograph. "I will tie a knot in my stringamejip to letter you with my silky paper, as I am given now to understand it will be worth my price in money one day" (458.26).

Regarded from a secular point of view, the Crucifixion is an atrocity, a brutal incident involving scourging, nailing to the cross, and intense thirst. This violence in III.2 is purely verbal and is spoken by Jaun himself, who treatens Issy in sadistic language echoing "Circe": "Holy gun, I'll give it to you, hot, high, and heavy before you can say sedro!" (439.5). Another passage darkly suggests scourging, nailed hands, and operatic screams. "I feel spirts of itchery outching out from all over me and only for the sludgehummer's force in my hand to hold them the darkens alone knows what'll who'll be saying of next. However. Now, before my upperotic rogister, something nice" (439.22). In another passage the nailing to the cross is described as the noise of a doorknocker ("moidhered by the rattle of the doppeldoorknockers" [445.31]).

As in the previous chapter, Jaun is reluctant to leave ("Pursonally, Grog help me, I am in no violent hurry. . . . I'd ask no kinder of fates than to stay where I am" [449.4, 449.12]). Like Christ, he asks the women not to weep for him ("So now, I'll ask of you, let ye create no scenes in my poor primmafore's wake" [453.2]). He tells someone, presumably the good thief, that when the clouds clear, they will find themselves in the Elysian fields ("Fieldnights eliceam, *élite* of the elect" [453.32]). Finally, he takes unsentimental leave ("So for e'er fare thee welt! Parting's fun" [454.1]), and the guards seem to thrust a lance in his side ("Something of a sidesplitting nature must have occurred to westminstrel Jaunathaun" [454.8]). However many identities he has, and one is surely the Paraclete, "Dave the Dancekerl," whom Jaun appoints to console Issy, is also John, the beloved disciple to whom Christ entrusted his mother: "my darling proxy" (462.16), "we're the closest of chems" (464.3), "I love him. I love his old portugal's nose" (463.18), "He's Jackot the Horner" (465.3). "In the beginning was the gest he jousstly says, for the end is with woman" (468.5).

Neither a novelistic portrait of Shaun/Jaun nor evidence of a negative identification with Christ in itself addresses the central issues of the three chapters of Book III. The form of these chapters is troublesome because there is very little action except the barrel tumbling into the water. Instead, we have questions and answers, less formal than the quiz show (I.6) and less informal than the washerwomen's gossip. Jaun's sermon to the girls resembles all his earlier lectures and sermons, complete with hypocritical and arrogant advice. Even so, the form suggests the matter: probes into sins and guilt and their aggressive defenses and into culpable family relationships. In short, the "watches" of Shaun are of a piece with the rest of *Finnegans*

Wake. The elements and structures of the Mass and the *via crucis* in the chapters help to clarify certain issues by introducing an antipode.

Shaun's function in the great Wakean scandal is to carry the letter that will exonerate HCE. The Christian act of salvation likewise serves to eradicate the effects of the Original Sin. But while the cross that Christ bears represents his acceptance of the sins of the world, Shaun's reluctance and virulent accusations against his brother illustrate the vehement defense against guilt that propels much of the action and speech in the work.

The New Testament replaces the authoritarian confrontation of God and man with the fraternal bond represented in the imagery and language of the Gospels. The themes of Christ's teachings, with their emphasis on reconciliation and forgiveness, are maliciously parodied in the fable of the Ondt and the Gracehoper (414–19), which, like a reversed parable of the prodigal son, is presented as a Gospel of sorts at the Mass, or like a politician's justification for a vote against welfare programs. Like postmen, priests deliver letters or epistles at Mass, but Shaun violently objects to reading letters from his brother about his father, or from the apostles and disciples about God ("those shem-letters patent for His Christian's Em" [419.19]), calling them "harro-brew bad . . . Puffedly offal tosh . . . all about crime and libel" (419.27, 32, 33). Priests and politicians alike receive contributions of money, and Shaun here, too, becomes defensive and belligerent, accus-ing the previous officers, "nettlesome goats" (412.28), of having eaten much "privet stationery and safty quipu" (412.27) out of "pension greed" (412.29). He goes on to claim, "I never spont it. . . . It went anyway like hot pottagebake" (414.8), and tries to divert the people by offers of a barrel of Guinness (perhaps the wine presented during the Offertory of the Mass).

Fraternal love as a Christian concept, expressed in the monastic relationships of Brothers and Sisters, is exploited in *Finnegans Wake* for its incestuous potential. Jaun, as priest addressing his "Sister dearest" (431.21), sounds on the surface not much different from Father Arnall in *Portrait* addressing "my dear little brothers in Christ" (*P*, p. 109). The erotic tone of Jaun's sermon in III.2 is further amplified by the animation of another pun, the dual meaning of "passion" as agony and lust—tempted to become a "passionate father" (457.6), Jaun evokes both *amour* and the religious order. Furthermore, Jaun becomes the embodiment of all the hypocritical lechery once projected onto Father

Moran by Stephen Dedalus in his jealousy over Emma Clery: "He had done well to leave her to flirt with her priest, to toy with a church which was the scullerymaid of christendom" (*P*, p. 220).

Although Joyce's use of Eastern religions as structuring elements in the *Wake* seems to have received greater study, the three "Shaun" chapters are controlled by Christian elements put to outrageously profane uses. This particular brand of sacrilege, which exploits various sexual and biological connotations in Christian themes and imagery, can be found abundantly in Mulligan's irreverence in *Ulysses*—"The Ballad of Joking Jesus," for example. Aside from questions of Joyce's personal religious attitudes, which seem largely irrelevant, there are a number of interesting justifications for this type of profanity in the *Wake*.

In a book ruled and structured by contraries, sacred versus profane, spiritual versus sensual, and exalted versus debased, all serve as important dichotomies. Beyond that, the Church reinforces societal taboos and repressions to an extreme degree. It is patriarchal and ascetic, and the celibacy of its clergy is an absolute extension of the incest taboo. Since they belong to the Divine Father, religious Mothers, Fathers, Brothers, and Sisters are forbidden to marry not only each other but anyone at all. *Finnegans Wake* depicts the breakdown of society at the level of the family and therefore utilizes sacrilege to dramatize the fall of the father and the failure of the father-son.

Finnegans Wake is also a dream-work, a basically Freudian dream-work, as I hope to show in later chapters. Conventional pieties and religious restraints are under siege in the world of the dream, where precisely those desires and forbidden wishes that are barred in waking thought strive to make themselves felt. Religious themes and imagery are particularly useful for the dreamer because the dream censor admits them readily. And yet, as Mulligan and authors of countless dirty religious jokes have discovered in the past, these same religious motifs offer ample opportunity for sexual double entendres and interpretations, and imaginative erotic and scatological elaborations.

The debasement of the life of Christ in the *Wake* both secularizes and humanizes it. Christ calling disciples to share his mission (Jaun urging Issy to engage in some good works) takes on all the naïve enthusiasm of an egotistical social worker. "Slim ye, come slum with me and rally rats' roundup! . . . Let us, the real Us, all ignite in our prepurgatory grade as aposcals and be instrumental to utensilise, help our Jakeline sisters clean out the hogshole and generally ginger things up. Meliorism in massquantities" (446.27, 36). Like a brisk sociologist requesting a case history, he asks for a report on infant mortality and indoor plumbing, or Herod's slaughter of the innocents and John Harington's water closet[12] ("mortinatality in the life of jewries and the sludge of King Haarington's at its height" [447.8]). Christ's healing becomes a call for hospitals ("When's that grandnational goldcapped dupsydurby houspill coming with its vomitives for our mothers-in-load and stretchers for their devitalised males?" [448.14]). But after all is said and done, this practical Jaun/Christ thinks of quitting unless he gets "an increase of automoboil and footwear" (448.29) as well as more money ("honest to John, for an income plexus that that's about the sanguine boundary limit. Amean" [448.32]). Shaun resembles Christ only in the structure of his actions, not in their meaning. He eats before walking, but with vulgar relish—not sacramental sharing. He is grumpy about bearing his involuntary cross. He tries to seduce Veronica, who will probably turn a fine profit from her bloody relic.

Other Wakean figures share the structure of Christ's life, if not his qualities. HCE, for example, is envied, slandered, and betrayed like Christ, and finally brought to trial, executed, and resurrected. That both Shaun and HCE share these functions involves no contradiction since, like Christ, who is his own father, and Hamlet, who is his own father (according to Stephen), a dreamer can also play father and son simultaneously in his dream.

Only by abandoning the novelistic approach to *Finnegans Wake* can readers free themselves from waking conventions and logic enough to enjoy the wholly imaginative reality of a dream-work. That this is not an inferior reality we know from Freud, whose neurotic patients lived enthralled to their psychic lives, and from Joyce's own Ulysses, whose intellectual and psychological odyssey makes the travels of Homer's hero pale by comparison. By abandoning conventional frames of reference, readers can allow the work to disclose its own meanings, which are lodged in the differences and similarities of its multitudinous elements.

2

THE NARRATIVE STRUCTURE

THE FUNCTION OF REPETITION

No better description of reading *Finnegans Wake* can be found than William York Tindall's comment on the hen's letter scratched from the dump: "for the first time we get a look at the text, such as it is, word for word, letter by letter. Our problem is what to make of what we have looked at."[1] To make something of what we have looked at, we irresistibly turn to familiar concepts of structure for a key to the "chaosmos" of *Finnegans Wake*. Intuitively, the reader may sense that these familiar notions of structure do not apply to this work, yet our entire epistemology has taught us to think of structure in terms of "anchors" or points of reference that constitute a center of the work.

Two predominant models have governed attempts to define the *Wake*'s structure. The first, despite Joyce's disavowal of structural similarities between *Finnegans Wake* and *Ulysses,* is the familiar plan of *Ulysses,* which brought that work into such immediate focus after the publication of Stuart Gilbert's book, *James Joyce's "Ulysses."* The second model, apparently sanctioned by Joyce via Samuel Beckett's essay in *Our Exagmination,* is a scheme of cyclical recurrence based on the *Scienza Nuova* of Giambattista Vico. The Ulyssean plan is anchored on a naturalistic narrative line, Bloom's day in Dublin. A corresponding literal line, a day in the life of Dublin pubkeeper H. C. Earwicker, serves as the primary point of reference both in Campbell and Robinson's *A Skeleton Key to "Finnegans Wake"* and Clive Hart's *Structure and Motif in "Finnegans Wake."* However, in order to accommodate Joyce's own suggestion that *Finnegans Wake* is a night piece, the work had to be formulated as both novel and dream by these critics. Clive Hart's scheme illustrates this combination most simply: while the entire work is a dream, the content of the dream is a naturalistic story.[2] To put it another way, *Finnegans Wake* is a dream about a novelistic story. Yet novels and dreams are based on fundamentally different approaches to reality. Novels are rooted in eighteenth-century empiricist notions of a unitary consciousness, while dreams are disguised messages from a censored unconscious.

Since it schematizes collective rather than individual experience, Beckett's Viconian model of the *Wake* does not share the novelistic premises of most later criticism. However, like the interpretations of Campbell/Robinson and Hart, the Viconian plan is also historical in its foundation on the linear progress of events through time. The movement is both cyclical and evolutional: events, though repeated at the end of the cycle, unfold in a logical and necessary sequence.[3] Such evolutional progress is difficult to discern in the *Wake*. For example, both the battle of Waterloo early in the book (I.1) and the nighttime stirrings of the Porter family near the end (III.4) represent the sexual dynamics of the family, the particular incestuous engagements that precipitate the fall of the father. Yet the expected political, moral, and linguistic modulations that express the progress of Vico's ages from Theocracy to Anarchy, from Birth to Decay, are not to be found in these episodes. The banal domestic sexuality of the Porters is no more corrupt or anarchic than the bawdy, raucous skirmish of Willingdone and the lipoleums. Nor do we find the expected stylistic correspondence to the Viconian ages. The bedroom sequence is not told in philosophical language, nor is the Museyroom battle described in sacred words. Structurally, the two events are virtually identical: the rebellious children rise against the father, and the father threatens the sons and tempts the daughter with his phallus, the "wounderworker" with "sexcaliber hrosspower" in the Museyroom (8.35–36), and the "drawn brand" (566.24) in the nursery. The brother relationship is likewise identical in nursery or adult confrontation. The passage of time separating the Mutt-Jute exchange on the prehistoric mound, the fifth-century debate between St. Patrick and the archdruid, and the twelfth-century quarrel of Mookse and Gripes has wrought no perceptible change. This aspect of the Wakean universe can be compared to Lévi-Strauss's "cold societies" or "peoples without history," who "make it the case that the order of temporal succession should have as little influence as possible on their content."[4]

Joyce's own literary evolution traces a gradual abandonment of diachronic structures in his novels. The very nature of *Portrait* requires an evolutional development: each event marks the progress of Stephen's psychological retreat from his origins—sunderings that will permit the poetic *rapprochement* with his heritage. In *Ulysses* the possibilities of a time that is simultaneously reversible and irreversible are further explored by contrasting Bloom's literal movements, as restricted by time (day) and space (Dublin), with the untrammeled confines of his consciousness. In *Finnegans Wake* unilinear time is abandoned even further. Marcel Brion writes of the events in *Finnegans Wake*, "Sometimes it even seems that the planes exist simultaneously in the same place and are multiplied like so many 'over-impressions'."[5] Brion suggests a synchronic or cross-sectional expression of history in the *Wake*, a concern with the persistence of identical structures in the various time planes of the work rather than with the effects of progress. Vico's emphasis on recurrent social states, therefore, contributes more significantly to the structure of the *Wake* than does his belief in ineluctable evolution. The recurrent events, however, though "presenting varied faces in different lightings and movements,"[6] do not represent historical cross-sections that are static—a series of frozen tableaus or movie stills, to use Lévi-Strauss's image. Each reenactment of a scene, whatever its imaginative "reality," is dynamic; each brother confrontation is still antagonistic, virulent, and tense. In other words, the repeated events themselves constitute temporal narratives: the washerwomen (I.7) do the laundry, chat about Anna, bicker, pick up the drying clothes at dusk, and go home. Later in the book the event is repeated: the boys in the nursery (II.2) do their homework (family history is found in school texts as well as in dirty linen), gossip about their mother, fight, close their lesson with a night letter, and presumably go to bed. This type of repetition does not appear to be merely predetermined like Vico's events, which repeat themselves because the logical progression of evolutionary change brings each cycle to a close in precisely the same condition as it began. Rather, the repetition in *Finnegans Wake* appears to be compulsive, that is, produced by irrational rather than logical necessity, and therefore actively induced—the result of human impulse rather than time. There is ample reason to consider the possibility that the repetition of events is generated by the pressure of an unresolved conflict, a mysterious trauma whose pain has never been relieved.

Joyce himself gives us a striking interpretation of thematic repetition in the "Scylla and Charybdis" episode of *Ulysses.* Stephen's analysis of Shakespeare's life and works insistently blurs the distinctions between the biographical and fictional reality of the author and couches in the language of classical criticism what is essentially a description of neurosis.

The note of banishment . . . sounds uninterruptedly from *The Two Gentlemen of Verona* onward till Prospero breaks his staff, buries it certain fathoms in the earth and drowns his book. It doubles itself in the middle of his life, reflects itself in another, repeats itself, protasis, epitasis, catastasis, catastrophe. It repeats itself again when he is near the grave, when his married daughter Susan, chip of the old block, is accused of adultery. But it was the original sin that darkened his understanding, weakened his will and left in him a strong inclination to evil. (*U,* p. 212)

This analysis suggests that an original trauma, repressed and barred from consciousness because of its associated guilt, becomes the source of a neurotic symptom. Shakespeare compulsively repeats certain themes in his writings without recognizing in these structures the concealed message of his own unconscious—"untaught by the wisdom he has written or by the laws he has revealed" (*U,* p. 197).

While Shakespeare's original sin is clearly identified as the youth's original submission to Ann Hathaway's seduction, the original sin in *Finnegans Wake* is never isolated from the welter of alternate versions, myths, and speculative accounts offered throughout the book. At no point does an account of the Phoenix Park incident qualify as the "real" or factual event, the "true" account of what happened that day. Instead, we merely receive many different versions with unmistakable structural similarities; specifically, each version reveals a particular set of relationships among a familial group of men and women. The lack of an authentic source, of a "true" version, suggests that the original sin, the original trauma, was itself experienced as a fiction or myth at the moment of its occurrence. In other words, as the trauma is lived, it is thought and subjected to language and therefore continues in consciousness as something other than its empirical or factual reality—as a myth.

The value of adopting this particular view of the Phoenix Park incident is that it permits us to relate the lack of a "true" account of the incident to the replication of themes in the work. Lévi-Strauss writes:

The traumatizing power of any situation cannot result from its intrinsic features but must, rather, result from the capacity of certain events, appearing within an appropriate psychological, historical, and social context, to induce an emotional crystallization which is molded by a pre-existing structure. . . . For the neurotic, all psychic life and all subsequent experiences are organized in terms of an exclusive or predominant structure, under the catalytic action of the initial myth.[7]

In other words, the original fictionalization of the trauma and the later compulsive behavior are both governed by the structuring function of the unconscious.

In Clive Hart's dream layers, the unconscious is depicted as full, as *content,* as a repository of hidden anxieties, forgotten memories, and the totality of personal history that becomes available to the conscious mind of the subject as he simply sinks deeper into sleep. In contrast, structuralists like Lévi-Strauss and Jacques Lacan have urged the reconsideration of these psychic processes in terms of language, by distinguishing the "preconscious" as the storage place of the individual's peculiar history, the personal vocabulary or lexicon, as it were, and the unconscious proper as the function by which laws are imposed on this vocabulary to make it grammatically meaningful. "The unconscious, on the other hand, is always empty—or, more accurately, it is as alien to mental images as is the stomach to the foods which pass through it. As the organ of a specific function, the unconscious merely imposes structural laws upon inarticulated elements which originate elsewhere— impulses, emotions, representations, and memories."[8] This concept applies equally to myth, dream, and neurotic symptom, all structures governed by unconscious laws. By examining *Finnegans Wake* in the light of these concepts, we can overcome the tendency to look for its meanings in its content, in the details of the events, and in the obscure allusion. Instead, the replication of events itself becomes meaningful and can be taken into account in a way that Hart's dream levels and Campbell and Robinson's literal narrative approach preclude.

The homology of myth and neurotic symptom further permits an invaluable correlation of social and personal experience. Joyce valued Vico as a social historian who provided him with new myths of origin. At the same time, Vico failed to provide Joyce with an individual psychology to complement his social theories. That Joyce desired such a fusion of the personal and the social is evident in the famous image of *Finnegans Wake* as "the dream of old Finn, lying in death beside the river Liffey and watching the history of Ireland and the world—past and future—flow through his mind."[9] By treating myth as the collective equivalent of the individual neurosis, we also become relieved of the burden of segregating mythic and naturalistic events in the *Wake;* the psychic mechanics of epic battles and children's quarrels are the same.

FORM AND THE OEDIPUS MYTH

As the Daedalus myth governs *Portrait,* and the Odyssey *Ulysses,* so *Finnegans Wake* is founded on the involuted patterns of the Oedipus myth. Joyce had previously circumscribed the family in his fiction: Stephen's flight and Bloom's travels and return mark the stress of opposing forces that bind the individual uneasily to the home. *Finnegans Wake* explores the nature of the family itself, via a quest for the original sin. All oedipal concerns are plumbed in the process—the mystery of identity, of sexual and social origin, and of the nature of man's relationship to God. If *Portrait* may be called the book of the Son and *Ulysses* the book of the Father, then *Finnegans Wake* is surely the book of the Holy Spirit, the hypostatic bond that unites them.

The quest serves as both form and content in *Finnegans Wake,* as structural principle and theme. Wakean speakers are ever seeking something, asking questions, investigating a mystery, gossiping, or speculating about this and that. Yet these same postures of inquiry and argumentation, slander, and the like perversely reveal the very information that is sought. For example, we know that one aspect of the original sin, of the fall of HCE, is the usurpation of the father's position by the sons. In I.2, the drunken citizens' attempt to discover HCE's guilty secret leads them to a symbolic act of aggression against HCE: the theme of "The Ballad of Persse O'Reilly" is parricidal, as is the act of writing the ballad itself. In II.3, the pub customers hear another account of the parricidal incident (Buckley and the Russian General, in this case) on the radio. They turn on HCE with accusations and recriminations, thereby reenacting the paternal conflict of the Butt and Taff skit.

A reference to the Oedipus myth helps to clarify the significance of this intricate fusion of form and content. Oedipus, in his quest for the murderer of Laius, seeks to close a discrepancy or gap that exists between what he knows and what he recognizes. He knows all the essential facts at the outset: the prophesy, his deeds, the events at Thebes just prior to his coming. He has simply failed to put them together, to see their correspondence and thereby recognize himself as the murderer whom he seeks.

Such a discrepancy between knowledge and recognition also constitutes the quest in *Finnegans Wake.* The answers to various riddles in the *Wake,* for example, are invariably contained in the relationship of the figures among whom the riddle is posed. The answer to the Prankquean's riddle, "Why do I am alook alike a poss of porterpease?" (21.18), resides in ALP and her relationship to her family, whether as mother of identical twins, as Tindall suggests,[10] or as bearer (porter) of peace, or as server of peas, like Rachel preparing the pottage for her sons' exchange. During the children's twilight games before the pub (II.1), Glugg fails to guess the correct color of the riddle—heliotrope. While he guesses the colors of insects and jewels, the rainbow girls dance around Chuff, their angel, in "heliolatry" (237.1), signaling the answer by the configuration of their relationship to the boy.

The impetus that occasions the quest in *Finnegans Wake,* as well as in the Oedipus myth and in psychoanalysis, is an inexplicable symptom: a mysterious plague brings barrenness and misery to Thebes, the neurotic suffers from unaccountable anxieties and compulsions, and the father, giant, and empire-builder falls in *Finnegans Wake.* In one specific instance, HCE's stammering denial to the cad's seemingly harmless question constitutes a neurotic symptom of a hidden conflict. The stutter and the vehemence of the incongruous defense point to the ancient crime, which the citizenry will make it their business to explore. Hosty, a type of HCE himself (at least, according to Tindall), will lead the prosecution, as Oedipus conducts his vigorous, unwitting investigation into his own past. Elsewhere, the fall of the father prompts the search for the ancient sin. ("What then agentlike brought about that tragoady thundersday this municipal sin business?" [5.13].) The quest is conducted in order to understand the cause of the symptom and, with the aid of this understanding, to effect a cure.

The search for the original sin leads inevitably to the heart of the family in the complex system of erotic and power relationships that bind the members into a primordially guilty union. The analogy to neurosis and the oedipal family is appropriate. The infantile trauma involves some permutation of sex and violence—perhaps the primal scene in which the erotic and the dangerous merge in a seeming struggle, or perhaps the wish to kill the father and marry the mother that derives its name from the Oedipus myth. In *Finnegans Wake* the quest yields just such guilty sexual and aggressive involvements: father versus son/sons, brother versus brother, father and son competing for sister/mother, brothers competing for sister/mother, as well as homosexual possibilities involving father and sons.

Buried under this disgraceful welter of family loves and hates lies the identity of the individual in society. Insofar as the individual is defined as the locus of numerous familial relationships, the violation of the incest taboo and those laws that ensure the peaceful succession of the son jeopardize the certainty of identity. Oedipus's quest leads from questions of a specific crime and specific guilt to the ultimate question, "Who am I?" The shifting, uncertain nature of characters in *Finnegans Wake* has long been recognized and documented, "In short, the people of the *Wake,* all thousand and one of them, are members or projections of the family, aspects of H.C.E. and A.L.P., who, in a sense, are the only people of the *Wake* and in the world."[11] This pervasive cross-identification of characters, however, is more than simply the reduction of individuals to types. Since the various actions of *Finnegans Wake* precisely portray competition for coveted positions, notably the role of king, father, and subject, rather than object, the confusion of characters and the frequent inability to distinguish between father/son/ brother result from the primal crossing of forbidden boundaries in the arena of those primal family relationships that produce identity.

MYTH STRUCTURES IN THE DREAM

We expect to find harmonious, symmetrical structure in Joyce's work, particularly in *Finnegans Wake,* with its apparent circularity of the whole, division into four books, and cyclical Viconian model. Not unreasonably, therefore, critical attempts to conceptualize the structure of *Finnegans Wake* have tended primarily toward the geometric: Tindall's concentric circles, Hart's mandalas and parallel tables. The most immediately striking feature of the work's structure, however, is certainly the thematic replication—the persistence of stable relationships among characters whose protean forms remind one of the "shapeshifters" of myths and fairy tales in their ability to appear as human (Shem and Shaun), animal (Ondt and Gracehoper), inanimate (rock and stone, pieces of laundry), and even abstract (Justius and Mercius, space and time). Joyce explored the mutability of forms and substances from many perspectives in his earlier works: the "Proteus" chapter of *Ulysses*, metempsychosis, alchemy, Yeats's theory of personality, and the Eucharist. Transubstantiation and transaccidentation therefore become, in Joyce's works, the central mysteries of life at the heart of religion, science, psychology, and art. In dreams, the mystery of changes in form and substance is shifted to the linguistic realm. Dreams employ linguistic play made possible precisely by discrepancies of form and substance (meaning)—puns or homophones as words of identical form but different meaning, like symbols in a rebus. "Assassination" is, therefore, a politically motivated murder in dream, but one having to do with "ass" and "sin"—hence the implied buggery of the shooting of the Russian General.

In *Finnegans Wake,* Joyce explores transmutation thematically through recurring dramas and tales in which the "accidents" change but the "substances" remain the same—a phenomenon corresponding to dream devices as well as to the constitution of similar myths found in widely disparate cultures. Lévi-Strauss writes: "The function of repetition is to render the structure of the myth apparent."[12] His own procedure for determining the "slated" structure of myths[13] may therefore suggest a more valuable approach than the determination of a primarily geometric organization of the work.

The third chapter of *Finnegans Wake* lends itself particularly well to a modified version of structural myth study. The ongoing investigation into HCE's mysterious sin is conducted in dense fog and clouds, producing only further garbled and bizarre versions of the incident. Since myth consists of all its versions, according to Lévi-Strauss, there is no necessity for establishing a true or original version. A number of the variant accounts of the incident as reported in I.3 can therefore be compared and the structural similarities noted.

1) (51-52) Asked for an explanation while smoking his pipe during target practice, the "porty" obliges by telling about the "One," the "Compassionate, called up before the triad of precoxious scaremakers."

2) (55-56) Upon request, "the Archicadenus" asks his listeners to imagine they were "seasiders, listening to the cockshyshooter's evensong evocation of the doomed but always ventriloquent Agitator" tearfully pointing his gun at the "leadpencil" monument which will be his mausoleum.

3) (62.3) A tall man, carrying a parcel, has a revolver thrust in his face by a masked assailant.

4) (63-64) After drunkenly falling against a gatestone pier, a wretch claims he was merely opening a bottle of stout by hammering it against the gate, when Maurice Behan, awakened by the noise, came rushing out.

The following elements recur in the several versions of the tale: the threatening confrontation between two men, involving guns, shooting, gunshot noises, and liquor; the dress and origins of the principals, described as outlandish in the sense of foreign, alien, and bizarre; the time marked by the Angelus; and the peripheral influence of two women. None of these elements is particularly new; in fact, several correlate with the comprehensive version of the HCE-cad encounter in I.2 (35–36).

The encounter between the two men is clearly in the order of the father-son, native-invader, king-usurper confrontation. Compared to the two most comprehensive accounts of paternal conflict, the HCE-cad and Buckley–Russian General encounters, the incidents in I.3 modulate the differences between these extreme versions. In his encounter with the cad, HCE has a totally irrational fear of being shot and so defensively draws his own gun, yet Buckley, a son figure, does indeed shoot the haplessly defecating Russian General. In the I.3 versions, "porty," an HCE-cad composite (HCE-porter with a calabash or pipe, like the cad), tells his story of the Phoenix Park encounter ("the One . . . called up before the triad of precoxious scaremakers" [52.13]) while shooting at empty bottles of stout. In a later version, another composite figure is arrested for making a noisy racket; he either fell drunkenly against a "gatestone pier" (63.28) or hammered a bottle of stout against the gate to open it, producing "the norse of guns" (64.2). The two accounts are curious inversions of each other—empty stout bottles being shot at and full stout bottles being opened sounding like gunshots. Two intervening accounts involve more concrete threats: the gun aimed at the "lead-pencil" (56.12) (Wellington) monument and the revolver shoved in the tall man's ("humping a suspicious parcel" [62.28] suggests HCE's hunchback; tall man: giant, Finn) face with the threat "you're shot, major" (62.32).

These four versions of an alleged incident, which has many more accounts throughout the book ("there extand by now one thousand and one stories, all told, of the same." [5.28]), function not as historical or literal narrations but as psychological variations of a single fantasy. The "sin in Phoenix Park," the giant's fall, the hod-carrier's fall, the soldier/father's murder in battle—all these are facets of the father's fall, revealing a complex cluster of interrelated fears and guilts. The four versions of I.3 itemize some of these more closely. As noted, these versions dramatize the ambiguous danger that generates the tension of the HCE-cad encounter: the simultaneous fear of parricide and the self-protective impulse to shoot first. Both antagonists are also variously described as foreigners dressed in outlandish clothes, such as "porty" seeking asylum on the "stranger stepshore" (51.31), the first Humphrey in exile in his "elbaroom surtout" (52.25), the Agitator wearing a Moslem fez, the Waylayer from the "prow of Little Britain" (62.36), and Maurice Behan, here identified with the three soldier-sons and the sons of Noah by his "homp, shtemp and jumphet" (63.36–64.1) tread, sporting a Japanese obi. The details of dress and origin reinforce the native versus invader aspect of the paternal conflict. They also suit the oedipal nature of the confrontations—the fatal meeting of father and son as strangers who fail to recognize each other. Joyce previously explored the nonfatal variant of this motif—the failure of Telemachus to recognize his father, Odysseus—in *Ulysses.* Peripheral references to two girls suggest a further oedipal as well as Edenic (Lili: Lillith, Pamona Evlyn: Eve) aspect of the encounter: the woman as cause and catalyst in the conflict between father and son, God and man. The confrontations occur at evening, a moment of change in the daily cycle from light to dark, from day to night. The timing of the encounters by the Angelus bells recalls the Annunciation and further evokes the conception of the son, which in the natural scheme of things signals the eventual deposition of the father.

An assembly of the bundles of diverse elements yields the general theme of the father's violent reaction to the danger implicit for him in natural change. Joyce's interest in mutability focuses on the psychological consequences of one of the most common changes of form in life—growing old. Much has been written in *Wake* studies about the importance of cycles as an affirmation of life's orderly and inevitable circular progress. A concern for the nature of the human conflicts would demonstrate the extent to which natural change and the passing of the social order along lawful lines of succession generate disturbance and anxiety in Wakean figures.

The fall of the father is expressed in three forms: the drunken or physical fall, the parricide or sociopolitical fall, and the moral or sexual fall. Insofar as the latter two motifs are grounded in the ambiguous

attitude of father toward sons—his simultaneous fear and aggression—
the first motif of the drunken fall adds yet another psychological
perspective to these complex feelings of the aging father, sensitive to
the changes upon him. The drunken fall motif associates drinking with
climbing and building (cf. Tim Finnegan), the ambition of the creator.
As the "Bygmester Finn" passage at the beginning of the book (4.18–
5.4) makes clear, the father as builder engages in essentially phallic
activity: the erection of monuments to ensure his immortality. It is
activity designed to stem the inevitable cycle of time and change that
will bring age and death to the father and ascendance to the son. The
last attempts at building lead the desperate father to excesses that
expose his mortality: he climbs too high (Ibsen's Masterbuilder motif),
builds too high (Tower of Babel motif), and drinks too much of his
harvest (Noah theme). In the case of Noah the exposure is literal and
phallic; the weakness that Cham exploits in his ridicule of the father is
the old man's sexual impotence.

This kind of analysis of the relationship of replicated elements in
the work is perhaps more helpful to understanding the work's teleology
than the geometric representations that have dominated studies of the
book's structure in the past. The major advantage of the method is that
it determines the work's structure intrinsically, rather than extrinsi-
cally, through analogy to preexisting systems. Furthermore, it allows us
to regard Joyce's self-avowed structural sources, the theories of Vico
and Bruno, as structural principles or methods of operation, rather than
as models, plans, or patterns. For example, the more or less arbitrary
correspondence of Vico's cycles to each section of the Wake[14] does
little to enhance our understanding of what happens in those sections.
On the other hand, the four Viconian cycles, divine, heroic, human, and
the ricorso, deal with men's inevitable power relationships, their possible positions in a hierarchy of power, their movements from one status
to another within that hierarchy, and their ultimate entrapment within
the system. The principle of Vico's cycles, therefore, has a great deal to
do with the relationships of fathers, sons, and brothers as they rise and
fall in Finnegans Wake. The structural approach described and advo-
cated here will not yield neat charts, tables, or blueprints of the work.
Instead, the method permits study of the work's structure from perspectives other than the novelistic narrative or the geometric—
perspectives which as a whole suggest that the nature of structure is
itself the central issue of Finnegans Wake.

THE MYTHS OF TRESPASS

Joyce said he wanted to tell the story of this Chapelizod family in a new way. This has implied to many the possibility of discovering the way it really was. Traditionally, III.4 was believed to represent the waking reality, although the most natural prose, describing the most natural events, is found in ALP's monologue just prior to her last farewell. It is unnecessary to assume that any realistic or down-to-earth version of events in *Finnegans Wake* belongs either to a "waking" reality or to a "shallow" dream state close to waking reality. Freud reports realistic dreams as well as fabulous dreams, so it is possible for complex dream impulses to disguise themselves in natural events.

Many homey, naturalistic images in ALP's monologue turn out to be dream distortions of earlier images. For example, she says to her husband, "you must buy me a fine new girdle too, nolly. When next you go to the Market Norwall. They're all saying I need it since the one from Isaacsen's slooped its line" (621.17). Like Sara, delivering Isaac in her old age, ALP has lost her figure. Earlier, as the river Liffey, who also has trouble controlling her shape, she asks for a new river corset, *"but I badly want a brandnew bankside, bedamp and I do, and a plumper at that! For the putty affair I have is wore out"* (201.5).

Another example is the puzzling image of a man following her about with a fork, denied earlier as "no widower whother soever followed us about with a fork on Yankskilling Day" (618.25). But in her monologue she ascribes this incident to her father, "the fiercest freaky every followed a pining child round the sluppery table with a forkful of fat" (626.11). Perhaps ALP, as hen, has found her way onto the Thanksgiving or supper table, a notion compatible with cannibal/communion motifs elsewhere in the book. But the father with the fork clearly becomes cold, mad, "feary" Neptune in the end, threatening her with the raised trident ("I see them rising! Save me from those therrble prongs!" [628.4]).

ALP talks of the letter, as she and HCE sit by the seashore, "the site of salvocean. And watch would the letter you're wanting be coming may be. And cast ashore" (623.29). There appear to be two letters: one floating in the ocean like a letter in a bottle coming from Boston— "After rounding his world of ancient days. Carried in a caddy or screwed and corked. . . . With a bob, bob, bottleby" (623.36)—and the other buried in the earth like the one retrieved by the hen, or like the

Book of Kells. The nautical letter sounds much like the barrel Jaun hurled into the river. In fact, letter and barrel may both be one with Jaun, who, in best postman fashion, sticks a stamp to his forehead before leaping into the falls, "gummalicked the stickyback side and stamped the oval badge of belief to his agnelows brow" (470.29). Since they are both written by ALP, however, it seems not unreasonable to consider them the same letter: the incubation in the foul subterranean Shem-style dump over a long period of time and the delivery in a Shaun-like barrel over vast stretches of space as merely two versions of the same event. In any event, both letters bring peace. The letter buried "till a kissmiss coming" (624.6) is presumably responsible for ALP's Christmas armistice (11.14), while the Jaun/barrel/letter leaping into the river is hailed with cries of "Peace" in many languages by the twenty-nine "pacifettes" (470.36).

Solness's church spire and Finnegan's scaffold become a modest bungalow, "bankaloan cottage" (624.7) in ALP's monologue. In this simple rambling account of ALP first hearing her lover's call, then asking him to build her a home, Joyce once again evokes Vico's marriage myth—the thunderous voice of God, "Thy voice, ruddery dunner" (624.5)—commanding the couples into the caves and marriage, "buildn our bankaloan cottage there and we'll cohabit respectable" (624.7).

The thunder's voice is not ALP's only brush with divinity. In her final words she thinks of HCE, "bearing down on me now under whitespread wings like he'd come from Arkangels" (628.9), like Zeus disguised as the swan bearing down on Leda, or like the Holy Ghost as angel/bird impregnating Mary. The Leda analogy is particularly important because it fits the Earwicker family configuration: Leda and Zeus, their twin sons Castor and Pollux, and the temptress Helen, who causes the Trojan War.

The Leda reference also supports the notion that the letter buried in the midden heap is a fertile egg, seed, or semen with potential life. In the same chapter the letter is described as the hen's egg, "as sure as herself pits hen to paper and there's scribings scrawled on eggs" (615.9). In the natural monologue section, domestic old ALP finds a "lintil pea" and a "cara weeseed" (625.23) in the dustbin while in the preceding chapter, with its sordid details of slum life, it is a used condom that is swept away in the rubbish, to the delight of the gossiping charwoman and her friends. "Never divorce in the bedding the glove that will give you away. Maid Maud ninnies nay but blabs to Omama . . . (and what do you think my Madeleine saw?): this ignorant mostly sweeps it out along with all the rather old corporators" (586.5). The buried letter as a seed evokes the myth of Atem, who created the first twin gods by masturbating his seed into the primeval mud pile.[15]

Such distortions and correspondences as these abound in the work, and they can be interpreted individually. But they do not really add up to a meaningful whole without a macrocosmic structure to integrate all the disparate elements of the work. In the decentered world of the *Wake,* this structure is not a single myth, as in *Ulysses,* but a series of major myths of creation, sin, and redemption.

The myths that contribute most to the thematic structure of *Finnegans Wake* include the Oedipus myth, as related earlier, Old Testament stories, the Gospels, the Irish legends of Finn MacCool, the Egyptian myths of Isis and Osiris, Greek and Roman myths, including Zeus and Leda, Romulus and Remus, and the modern biography of Charles Parnell. At the heart of each is a crime, a violation—specifically, an act of trespass over a forbidden boundary. The trespass persists while the nature of the territory varies from myth to myth: knowledge, the prerogative of God, in the Eden myth; sex with the mother, the prerogative of the father, in the Oedipus myth; sex with the wife, the prerogative of the husband in the legends of Finn MacCool, Tristan and Isolde, and in the Parnell story. Imperialism or invasion is a literal act of trespass, as in the military campaign of Napoleon or the missionary conquest of St. Patrick. Stealing the birthright in the Jacob and Esau story, looking at forbidden parts in the voyeurism of the sons of Noah, and loving the "wrong" sex, as in the life of Oscar Wilde, all provide still other instances.

Implicit in these crimes, therefore, is the notion of laws, of boundaries, of an ordering of rights and duties and a legal organization of space. The nature of the violations is in one sense political, bringing about the kind of power shifts that propel Vico's cycles on their downward course. But Joyce introduced a particular Freudian aspect into the notion of trespass in *Finnegans Wake,* a series of guilty fantasies that arise from the crossing of boundaries that mark sexual taboos, forbidden areas of sexual exploration. Treated as part of the overall family dynamic, the themes of incest and parricide, voyeurism and exhibitionism, shooting and shitting, will be integrated in my next chapter with the other forms of trespass, such as military invasion, stealing, and lying, in a decentered vision of society. In searching for an original sin, Joyce seems to have activated all possible meanings of the Lord's Prayer—"forgive us our trespasses, as we forgive those who trespass against us."

Sins of trespass are also particularly suitable for a dream-work because the purpose of the dream is precisely that: to thrust forbidden thoughts or desires into the consciousness of the dreamer, against the defense of the dream censor who vigilantly guards against such invasion. It is interesting to consider the function of the constable in *Finnegans Wake* in the light of the dream censor. The constables in Joyce's earlier works, *Dubliners'* "Grace," and *Ulysses,* appear on the scene in order to help drunken men: Tom Kernan, who fell down the steps of the pub, and Stephen, fighting with the soldiers.

This involvement of constables with drunks suggests an explanation for the controversy about the constable's identity in the *Wake.* It is entirely plausible that the constable and the janitor of the pub are the same person, particularly since they are both "porters" of sorts—turnkey or gatekeeper as well as the person who sweeps, washes the bottles, and lights the lamps in the pub. In the dream the various meanings of a single word are often activated simultaneously. This principle also accounts for HCE being both a turnpiker and a pub-keeper, since "publican" means both. The precedent for a porter who is drunk is, of course, the famous gatekeeper in *Macbeth.* The porter in *Finnegans Wake* is also wakened by the knocking at the gate (64.2, 67.19) and is drunk and is the gatepost itself when Jaun leans against him in III.2 ("comestabulish Sigurdsen . . . equilebriated amid the embracings of a monopolized bottle"[429.19]).

It is the constable, however, who incarcerates people for their own protection. Like the watches who check on drunken Stephen after his brothel debauch, it is "petty constable Sistersen" (186.19) who saves Shem from the mob when he finds him "reeling more to the right than he lurched to the left, on his way from a protoprostitute" (186.25), and it is the "Sockerson boy" (370.30) who locks up the pub after the customers have virtually vanquished HCE ("Shatten up ship!" [370.34]). It is also some "faithful poorters" who "triplepatlockt" HCE for his own protection earlier in the work (69.25–26). The notion of a constable locking people away for their own protection is analogous to the function of the dream censor, who represses the (unconscious) dreamer in order to protect the (conscious) dreamer. The image of the locked gate is particularly appropriate for representing the defense against trespass and intrusion.

In each of his major works, Joyce uses myth not only as a template for shaping the chaos of modern life, as Eliot suggests, but also as a dramatic and narrative analogue to the psychological conflicts that beset all men at all times. The Dedalus myth of *Portrait* signifies the schism of the artist, suspended between the sightless humanity of the labyrinth and the blinded deity of the soaring angel. The Ulyssean dilemma of Bloom depicts the conflict of the exile torn between forgetful surrender to alien forces and the conquest of those psychological obstacles barring the repossession of home. Not monomythic, like the earlier works, *Finnegans Wake* uses Oedipal and Christian myths to plumb the conflict of the individual, confronted by primordial guilt, who is tempted to deny and confess, to evade and embrace responsibility for an involuntary, nonvolitional sin.

Like Kafka, Joyce relegates the treatment of an inexplicable guilt, a haunting persecution for a crime one does not remember, to the realm of nightmare. Even the witty fairy tale of the Prankquean contains numerous allusions to dire punishments for unspecified sins, probably of a sexual nature.[16] The kidnapping of children, like Grace O'Malley's reprisal against the Earl of Howth for closing the door against her, may also derive from a Grimm fairy tale, "Our Lady's Child": a young woman opens a forbidden door revealing the Holy Trinity and is punished with mutism and the abduction of each of her three children, two sons and an infant daughter, by Mary, the Mother of God.[17] Before each child is taken, the young woman is given an opportunity to confess, but like van Hoother, who can only say "Shut" in answer to the riddle, she remains silent. References to the avenging angel of the Passover recall the murder of the Egyptian firstborns as punishment for sins ("there was a brannewail that same sabboath night of falling angles" [21.24]). Allusions to Noah's flood and Moses' forty-year exodus through the wilderness refer to other instances of God's wrath.

The most significant element that *Finnegans Wake* shares with the Oedipus myth and the Christian cycle is the gap of consciousness between the sin and the atonement. Like Oedipus, who must atone for a crime committed unwittingly, and Christ, who atones for the sin of the first parents, Wakean figures suffer from guilty being rather than guilty acts, like HCE blamed for the misconduct of his parents ("Is that right what your brothermilk in Bray bes telling the district you were bragged up by Brostal because your parents would be always tumbling into his foulplace and losing her pentacosts after drinking their pledges?" [634.31]). Joyce is not an existential writer, nor, indeed, could he be as author of a dream-work. Like Bloom, who couldn't hurt a fly in waking life and yet fears "the committal of homicide or suicide during sleep by an aberration of the light of reason" (U, p. 720), dreamers are subject to the terror of Oedipus, who fears he may kill his father and marry his mother whether he wants to or not. Dreamers are confronted with crimes never committed or consciously willed, for which they must claim responsibility all the same.

The gap that separates the individual from recognition and acceptance of his guilt is spanned in dreams by the repressed childhood and racial memories that make their appearance like the messengers and witnesses at Oedipus's inquest. This accounts in part for the compressed and reversible time in *Finnegans Wake*. But the dream is only a symptom of repression, after all—a warning of unresolved conflicts that produces a momentary relief with their expression, if not their cure. A cure would require an act of consciousness: psychoanalysis to effect the cure of the oedipal trauma, or reception of the sacraments for Christian salvation. But in the dream the same obsessions and repressed desires will recur, in different guises, in order to make themselves known to the dreamer—like the drama reenacted nightly at the "Feenichts Playhouse" (219.2), with "nightly redistribution of parts and players by the puppetry producer and daily dubbing of ghosters" (219.7).

3

THE
THEMES

FAMILY AND SOCIETY

At the mythic heart of *Finnegans Wake* lies the model for all mythic designs—the human family. This family is Freud's oedipal family, a primal, law-governed unit in which the claims of society first impose themselves on the individual and are resisted in the interest of self-possession. Amid the catalogue of themes in the second paragraph of *Finnegans Wake,* the distinct oedipal elements of law and family conflict are presented in neat juxtaposition ("nor avoice from afire bellowsed mishe mishe to tauftauf thuartpeatrick: not yet, though venissoon after, had a kidscad buttended a bland old isaac: not yet, though all's fair in vanessy, were sosie sesthers wroth with twone nathandjoe"[3.9]). The unbegotten Yahweh announces His name to Moses from the burning bush—*mishe* is Gaelic for "I am"; *tauf,* the German word for baptize and christen, is followed by a reference to "Thou art Peter, . . ." Christ's simultaneous conferral of a new name and the temporal authority over the Church on Simon. Next is a reference to Jacob's deception of his blind father, Isaac, by which he stole the birthright from his twin brother, the goatherd Esau. In keeping with the particularly Irish allusions in the passage—"mishe," "Patrick" for "Peter," "peat" for "rock"—this segment also includes a reference to an Irish Isaac: Isaac Butt, who was replaced as head of the

41

Irish Party by the younger Charles Parnell. Finally, there is reference to a divided and reversed Jonathan Swift, "nathandjoe," whose amours with two girls, Esther Johnson (Stella) and Esther Vanhomrigh (Vanessa), form one of the basic configurations for a recurrent father-daughter incest motif throughout the work.

This family theme, which occurs throughout Joyce's works, consists of a series of oppositions in which the conflicting demands of the society and the individual are expressed. The Law is symbolically embodied in the father, actually in the name of the Father, as we shall see. The father's conferral of the birthright on his son preserves the hierarchy of authority that ensures the peaceful transition of the law through the generations. Joyce's allusion to the origin of the Church's hierarchy and authority in Christ's words, "Thou art Peter," indicates the function of the father as namer, or as designator of identity and position in the system over which he presides.[1] The identity and position of the son in this system of lawful descent is always pre-ordained, a condition upon which young Stephen in *Portrait* reflects as he reads the inscription in his geography text:

Stephen Dedalus is my name,
Ireland is my nation.
Clongowes is my dwellingplace
And heaven my expectation. (P, p. 16)

With his careful, child's logic, Stephen recognizes that God is non-contingent—not fixed in time, space, and identity like he is.

God was God's name just as his name was Stephen. *Dieu* was the French for God and that was God's name too; and when anyone prayed to God and said *Dieu* then God knew at once that it was a French person that was praying. But though there were different names for God in all the different languages in the world and God understood what all the people who prayed said in their different languages still God remained always the same God and God's real name was God. (P, p. 16)

The son's ability to conceive of himself as a center in the universe of his thought is impaired by his preordained position in the social order,[2] and a struggle for selfhood ensues in the form of a struggle with the father, the end of which is symbolic parricide. In Joyce's earlier works, the escape from the social bondage that stifles the individual and inhibits his creative powers is provided by the dream of exile. Stephen Dedalus in *Ulysses* redirects his struggle toward the symbolic father

("[*He taps his brow.*] But in here it is I must kill the priest and the king" [*U*, p. 589]).

The son's subordination to the father ensures not only the peaceful transmission of the law, but also the repression of incestuous impulses, which constitutes the primal law of the social order. According to modern anthropological theorists, the viability of the social group requires that systems of exchange within the society be subject to law. Culture comes into existence with the incest taboo, the substitution of "the mechanism of a sociologically determined affinity for that of a biologically determined consanguinity."[3] Just as the son's rebellion against the father disrupts the system of lawful descent, so incest disrupts the social structure by destroying the preordained order of lineages. This rudimentary outline of family function and structure suggests that the conflict between the individual and society resides in the opposition between lawful transference and exchange, and unlawful appropriation. The ritual forms of giving and taking in *Finnegans Wake* help to define the nature of familial relationships in the struggle for self-possession and, therefore, warrant closer study.

In *Finnegans Wake* an early preoccupation of Joyce's merges with a mature one. His interest in the problems of selfhood and his later concern with Viconian social theory required a vehicle for the simultaneous expression of psychoanalytic and social processes. This need was aptly filled by the Oedipus myth, which was familiar to Joyce from a number of perspectives, including the Freudian. In the Oedipus myth, private acts have public consequences, personal crimes become civic crimes, parricide is also regicide, and the quarrels between brothers-in-law threaten to result in civil war. Freudian psychology elaborates this myth in the theory that infantile instincts persist in the character of the adult, that familial relations express themselves collectively in the conduct of nations, and that colonial revolutions can therefore be treated as analogues of infantile patricidal wishes. Psychological conflicts are also often translated into religious impulses, so that filial disobedience becomes spiritual rebellion—as Joyce demonstrated in the earlier *Portrait*.

Civilization requires repression, and Joyce's earlier works explore the consequences of that repression in the spiritual paralysis of *Dubliners*, Stephen's artistic impotence in *Portrait*, and Bloom's sexual impotence in *Ulysses*. The first agency of repression is the family, so it is not surprising that when the strict conscience is relaxed, as in the hallucinatory ambience of Nighttown, it is the family members or their surrogates who rise in fantasy to torment Stephen and Bloom: Stephen's mother and the priests of his childhood, Molly Bloom with her lover, Bloom's father and dead son. But in Nighttown, Stephen strikes at his mother's ghoulish image with his ashplant, and Bloom indulges his most shameful erotic fantasies. In the dream world of *Finnegans Wake* the family also engages in the gamut of antisocial activities, including war, seduction, kidnapping, murder, invasion, stealing, lying, slander, forgery, and hypocrisy. The teleology of their universe is freedom, and in the enduring struggle between the individual's anarchic psyche and the laws that make civilization possible, the psyche is momentarily triumphant only in the dream.

THE PRIMAL SCENE

Finnegans Wake harbors at its center a myth of origins that functions as a living mystery for its figures. A secret source of guilt, like the theological Original Sin or the Freudian crimes of incest and parricide buried in the unconscious, its manifestation is an evasive and digressive narrative style. This quest for the "truth" of the ancient crime at the root of HCE's downfall yields verbal accounts, like the testimonies of Oedipus's messenger and shepherd, or the anamnesis of the psychoanalytic patient. In *Finnegans Wake* these take the form of rumors, scandal, interrogation, trials, analyses, and the like. From the varying details of many hypothetical versions and allusions, a basic configuration of the event emerges. The principals are always the same: an old man, two girls, and three soldiers—representatives of Earwicker and his children. The girls tempt the old man to commit assorted indecencies that the three men witness; in some versions, they then rise in battle against the father figure. These indecencies form an almost complete array of sexual perversions. According to Campbell and Robinson, "Butt's ambiguities and innuendoes fan out into a veritable Krafft-Ebing report of sexual depravity, implicating even Butt and his soldier companions in a mishmash of homo-hetero-anal-voyeur misconduct."[4]

The voyeuristic and exhibitionistic aspects of the event require special notice. The girls tempt the old man by their exposure while urinating, and his peeping at them causes his downfall ("the besieged bedreamt him stil and solely of those lililiths undeveiled which had undone him" [75.5]). HCE's voyeurism, paralleled by Charles Dodgson's hobby of photographing little girls, expresses his desire for his daughter Isabel, who appears in his dreams like Botticelli's Venus ("I reveal thus my deepseep daughter which was bourne up pridely out of medsdreams unclouthed when I was pillowing in my brime" [366.13]). In turn, HCE exposes himself to the girls. Even by ALP's well-intentioned account, he "dropped his Bass's to P flat" (492.3) and "showed me his propendiculous loadpoker" (493.10). The exhibition, however, is clearly for the benefit of his daughter Isabel, who in the bedroom/nursery sequence of the last chapter in Book III, looks upon her father's awesome erection ("The infant Isabella from her coign to do obeisance toward the duffgerent, as first futherer with drawn brand. . . . How shagsome all and beastful! What do you show on? I show because I must see before my misfortune so a stark pointing pole" [566.23]). The three soldier/sons of the Phoenix Park occurrence witness the old man's showing and viewing; like Kev and Dolph in the nursery, viewing the "whome" of their "eternal geomater" (296.36), they are Noah's sons, "mem and hem and the jaquejack" (422.33) to HCE, exposing the phallic secret of the father.

This inordinate emphasis on watching and being watched in the midst of sexual activity ("They were watching the watched watching" [509.2]), suggests that this primal sin is in fact a primal scene.[5] The "treefellers in the shrubrubs" (420.8) and "our maggy seen all, with her sisterin shawl" (7.32) are clearly the three little Earwicker children watching their parents' copulation.

Yet they wend it back . . . to peekaboo durk the thicket of slumbwhere, till their hour with their scene be struck for ever and the book of the dates he close, he clasp and she and she seegn her tour d'adieu, Pervinca calling, Soloscar hears. (O Sheem! O Shaam!), and gentle Isad Ysut gag, flispering in the nightleaves flattery, dinsiduously, to Finnegan, to sin again and to make grim grandma grunt and grin again. . . . (580.13)

The coincidence of primal sin and primal scene draws attention to several interesting complications of the fall in *Finnegans Wake*. An essential characteristic of both theological and psychoanalytic primal sins, the sin of Adam and the crime of Oedipus, is their legacy to progeny and populace: all men are born with the stain of Original Sin, and all will be guilty of oedipal wishes. An individual, private crime becomes a public, universal, and unconscious sin. This essential relationship between private and public acts, which is dramatized in the primal scene, forms a major theme in *Finnegans Wake*. HCE's sin is private and hidden, buried in the past, and perhaps even lost to consciousness. Yet the sin in Phoenix Park becomes a public matter, a "municipal sin business" (5.13), a scandal that dominates universal concern and conversation.

The primal sin, in both the Edenic and Oedipus myths, is the sin of usurping the prerogative of the father, be it acquisition of his knowledge, or appropriation of his throne and wife. The guilt engendered by the primal sin is of this order: the child watching the copulation of his parents learns the secret of procreation, a knowledge that will eventually enable him to replace the father as creator. This is the central teaching of the "Night Lesson" in the *Wake* (II.2).

> For, let it be taken that her littlenist is of no magnetude or again let it be granted that Doll the laziest can be dissimulant with all respects from Doll the fiercst, thence must any whatyoulike in the power of empthood be either greater THAN or less THAN the unitate we have in one or hence shall the vectorious ready-eyes of evertwo circumflicksrent searclhers never film in the elipsities of their gyribouts those fickers which are returnally reprodictive of themselves. (298.8)

This passage seems to involve dream reversal since it contains an obvious error. "Thence must any whatyoulike in the power of empthood be either greater THAN or less THAN the unitate we have in one ... " suggests that any number ("whatyoulike") raised to the power of zero ("power of empthood," 2^0, for example) must be greater or less than one. A number raised to the power of 0 is, of course, equal to 1. Since the entire paragraph comprises a theorem, we may assume that an error in one part also reverses other elements in the theorem. "Doll the laziest" (last) and "Doll the fiercst" (first) may be as identical as Isabel and her mirror image rather than $D_1 \neq D_2$. The last section of the theorem—which, as a whole, deals with parenthood ("power of empthood")—may therefore also be reversed. In other words, the voyeuristic twins ("vectorious": victorious, "ready-eyes" or "searclhers": searchers; also the radial ["ready-eye"] vectors of two flickering search lights or circles) may indeed be able to film the "elipsities" (lapses, ellipse: curve, ellipses: gaps) of the spiraling ("gyribout") movements of those "fickers" (fuckers, figures) that are "returnally" (eternally) "reprodictive" (reproductive, predictive) of themselves—their parents.

The passage suggests that it is not the erotic but the procreative aspect of parental copulation that intrigues the Earwicker children.

"The 'sin' in the sex act is not that of love but that of parentage," writes Norman O. Brown. "It is the father and the mother, not the lover and the beloved, who disappear from the highest Paradise."[6] Helmut Bonheim notes the same phenomenon in *Finnegans Wake.* "Even Adam and Eve seem to sin in *Finnegans Wake* as the parents of Cain and Abel rather than as the children of God. . . . Adam's guilt is associated not so much with disobedience as with fatherhood and age."[7] Of course, Adam's disobedience is itself a son's rebellion against the father; Adam hides the procreative phallus that has usurped God's prerogative ("Feigenbaumblatt and Father" [150.27]). The father engenders his own patricide by the begetting of sons. "Sonship and brotherhood are espoused against fatherhood: but without a father there can be no sons or brothers."[8] The attribution of the Original Sin to God, which James Atherton regards as a basic axiom of *Finnegans Wake,*[9] very likely refers to the father's responsibility for the self-destructive aspect of his creativity. If the parricidal wish is inevitable, then the father must murder his children or be murdered. Laius orders Oedipus exposed, Cronus eats his children, and HCE, like these analogues, has an "eatupus complex" (128.36), revealing his own cannibalistic designs on his children. The Earwicker sons' fear of the father is expressed as "a child's dread for a dragon vicefather" (480.25). It causes the nightmare of the infant Jerry who is assured by his mother, "You were dreamend, dear. The pawdrag? The fawthrig? Shoe! Hear are no phanthares in the room at all, avikkeen. No bad bold faathern, dear one" (565.18). But murderous intentions are reciprocal in the Oedipal family. The boys plot parental death and burial while their parents copulate ("and the youngfries will be backfrisking diamondcuts over their lyingin underlayers, spick and spat trowelling a gravetrench for their fourinhand forebears" [572.3]).

TRIANGULAR DESIRE

While the father-son conflict operates at a visceral level in the nursery, around feelings of danger and self-preservation, the thematic development of their adult confrontations broadens into a complex dramatization of the struggle for selfhood in intersubjective relationships. The expression of both paternal and fraternal rivalry, through the models of imperialistic conflict and the love triangle, suggests that the male conflicts in *Finnegans Wake* are founded on a dialectic of desire that revolves around mediated objects.

The love triangle is a predominant theme in Joyce's work, even as early as the poem about the rival in *Chamber Music*. Joyce develops the jealous emotions engendered by competition for a beloved in the relationship of Stephen to Emma Clery and Father Moran in *Stephen Hero*. But not until *Exiles* does he also explore the homosexual and masochistic aspects of such affairs. *Exiles* is notable too for shifting the focus from the man-woman to the man-man relationship, thereby relegating the woman to a mediated position.

The triangular relationships in *Finnegans Wake* are developed most fully in the children's games of II.1 and the Tristan/Isolde chapter, II.4. Other love triangles occur in parables and fables, for example, the tale of Burrus, Caseous, and Margareen. But the unmistakable oedipal configuration of these affairs is best revealed in the myth of King Mark's betrayal by Tristan and Isolde, and in its analogue, the legend of Finn MacCool, Dermot, and Grania. Tristan and Dermot are nephews of the older men, or sons by displacement; the women they *steal* are bride and wife, respectively, of Mark of Cornwall and Finn MacCool. Among the many permutations of the oedipal triangle in *Finnegans Wake,* the father's position as an obstacle to the son's desire for the mother is clearly a factor. Yet the Tristan myth in the *Wake* emphasizes the wish to replace the father as King; the stealing of his bride seems to be a means to that more primary objective. The chapter devoted to the Tristan myth (II.4) opens with a verse or song mocking the defeated, impotent, old king.

—*Three quarks for Muster Mark!*
Sure he hasn't got much of a bark
And sure any he has it's all beside the mark.
. . . .
You're the rummest old rooster ever flopped out of a Noah's ark
And you think you're cock of the wark.
Fowls, up! Tristy's the spry young spark
That'll tread her and wed her and bed her and red her
Without ever winking the tail of a feather
And that's how that chap's going to make his money and mark! (383.1)

The subordination of the love affair to the father-son conflict is suggested by the reference to Mark as a drunken Noah, recalling the encounter of HCE and the three sons in the Phoenix Park incident and the pun on "mark" itself ("beside the mark" versus "make his money and mark"), indicating the son's usurpation of the father's position. Since Isolde is clearly desired by the son because she is also desired by the father, her position is mediated in the quarrel between father and son. René Girard, who reveals this same configuration of "triangular desire" at the thematic core of the novels of Flaubert, Stendhal, Proust, and Dostoyevsky, points out that the motivating principle of this type of love relationship is the subject's imitation of the desire of the other, in order to be like him, to become him.[10]

Not only do love triangles often have political consequences, as young Stephen Dedalus learns over a spoiled Christmas dinner, but the same competitive dynamics that prompt rivalry in love also prompt rivalry in war. Joyce features those military conflicts in *Finnegans Wake*—Clontarf, Balaklava, Waterloo—that are marked not only by imperialistic consequences, but also by strong interpersonal rivalries that simulate paternal and fraternal conflicts: King Sitric and Brian Boru, Lord Lucan and Captain Nolan, Wellington and Napoleon. Like little Tommy and Jacky Caffrey battling over the sand castle in *Ulysses,* or young Stephen competing in math class under the silk badges of York and Lancaster, military disputes are motivated in Joyce's works by a desire for dominance both stronger and more complex than the mere desire for possession. ("This is hiena hinnessy laughing alout at the Willingdone. This is lipsyg dooley krieging the funk from the hinnessy" [10.4]). The slapstick wargames of the *Wake*'s mock Waterloo battle test the manhood of each participant in the face of raucous humiliation. The battles between males in the *Wake* have the earmarks of the classic Master-slave dialectic of Hegelian philosophy. According to Kojève, Hegel's definition of man's humanity rests upon a distinction between his animal "desire," which is directed toward objects, and his human "Desire," which is directed toward another "Desire." "Therefore, to desire the Desire of another is in the final analysis to desire that the value that I am or that I 'represent' be the value desired by the other: I want him to 'recognize' my value as his value. I want him to 'recognize' me as an autonomous value. . . . Therefore, to speak of the 'origin' of Self-Consciousness is necessarily to speak of a fight to the death for 'recognition'."[11] Hegel's fight to the death for "recognition" devolves into the Master-slave dialectic, which Norman O. Brown attributes to the father-son relationship. "The dispute between fathers and sons is over property . . . paternal power is a property which is inherited and which consists in having property in one's own children. To be the subject of a king is the same as to be the son of a father; and to be a son is the same as to be a slave."[12]

Significantly, the most overt act of parricide in *Finnegans Wake,* Buckley's shooting of the Russian General, finds the warring sons united in the aspects of the newly liberated ("BUTT and TAFF [*desprot slave wager and foeman feodal unsheckled, now one and the same person. . . .*]" [345.7]). The objective of parricide is a noncontingent selfhood, an identity with appurtenant rights and powers not subject to bequest, but wrenched violently from the father by the unlawful appropriation of his wife, property, and life; having killed the father, the slave/son comes into possession of himself.

The fraternal rivalry in *Finnegans Wake* is also patterned on the Hegelian dynamic of the father-son conflict. Campbell and Robinson comment on the brothers' opposition, "If it is the typical lot of Shem to be whipped and despoiled, Shaun is typically the whipper and despoiler."[13] Although the brothers are presented as equal opposites and therefore interchangeable ("Galliver and Gellover. Unless they changes by mistake. I seen the likes in the twinngling of an aye" [620.13]), their relationship consists of a power struggle. Shaun's shrill denunciation of Shem as a sham (I.7) whose "lowness" is the hallmark of his character, employs the strategy of the Hegelian Master, who maintains his authority over the slave by refusing to grant him "recognition." In the fable of the Mookse and the Gripes, it is precisely the humanity of his antagonist that the Shaun-like Mookse refuses to acknowledge, while demanding obeisance for himself ("Blast yourself and your anathomy infairioriboos! No, hang you for an animal rurale! I am superbly in my supremest poncif! Abase you, baldyqueens!" [154.10]).

The configuration of the enemy twins enjoys a dual function in expressing antagonistic relationships in the *Wake.* On one hand, the fraternal struggle reflects the same dynamic process of Hegelian intersubjective struggle as the father-son conflict. On the other hand, the Wakean enemy twins clearly constitute a divided self. The twins have their philosophical roots in Bruno's dualism ("every power in nature must evolve an opposite in order to realize itself"). This evolution of opposites is a dynamic struggle in *Finnegans Wake,* a process of simultaneous identification and aggression in which the chief weapon is unlawful appropriation.

The relationship of Shem and Shaun as a divided self is always implied and can be found stated explicitly in some passages. "He's the sneaking likeness of us, faith, me altar's ego in miniature. . . . I'm enormously full of that foreigner, I'll say I am! Got by the one goat, suckled by the same nanna, one twitch, one nature makes us oldworld kin. . . . I hate him about his patent henesy, plasfh it, yet am I amorist. I love him" (463.6). Foreign and old world kin—this relationship has psychoanalytic resonances, like Oedipus and Laius in bloody combat at the crossroads as ostensible aliens, but really father and son. As the relationship of the doubled self, it has intrasubjective resonances as well, for the experience of being simultaneously oneself and a stranger— even an enemy—to oneself, describes the experience of the infant first confronted with its mirror image. French psychoanalyst Jacques Lacan calls this primordial event in the child's life the *stade du miroir*. This first confrontation with his mirror image is an alienating experience for the child, because for the first time he perceives himself as an object, an "other," an image of an "I" that is "me." This alienation from the self as "other" results in aggressivity with the intent of appropriating or controlling the "other" self.[14]

The *Wake*'s enemy twins as mirror image antagonists are even represented by mirror-reflected typographical symbols ("Here [the memories framed from walls are minding] till wranglers for wringwrowdy wready are, Fꟼ" [266.20]).[15] According to Lacan, the child will be enthralled to his "other" until he can reclaim his own subjectivity, his sense of himself as subject rather than object. This liberation comes with the acquisition of language, which Lacan characterizes as an act of appropriation, of taking for one's own.[16] By acquiring language, the child can participate in the world as speaker rather than spoken about, as namer rather than named, as judge rather than judged. He becomes assured of his control over his mirror image, because that alter ego cannot initiate speech.

The struggle between the mirror twins of *Finnegans Wake* involves many kinds of appropriation, including the theft of love and ambiguous exchanges of money reminiscent of the gold coin in "Two Gallants." But word-stealing plays the major role in the brother conflict. If Shem, the underdog, invariably bests his brother, it is precisely because his nefarious linguistic activity functions as an ineluctable threat. Shem is variously described as an eavesdropper and word-stealer, "treasuring with condign satisfaction each and every crumb of trektalk, covetous of his neighbour's word" (172.29); a would-be forger, who studies "how cutely to copy all their various styles of signature so as one day to utter an epical forged cheque on the public for his own private profit" (181.15); and a plagiarist ("Who can say how many pseudostylic shamiana, how few or how many of the most venerated public impostures, how very many piously forged palimpsests slipped in the first place by this morbid process from his pelagiarist pen?" [181.36]). Reference to Shem's writing as "some most dreadful stuff in a murderous mirrorhand" (177.30), provides the first clue that the victim of this thieving is his mirror-image twin—a suspicion seemingly confirmed by Shaun's blustering accusations before the four old men ("As often as I think of that unbloody housewarmer, Shem Skrivenitch, always cutting my prhose to please his phrase, bogorror, I declare I get the jawache!"[423.14]). However, when asked insistently about his own language and writing ability, Shaun reveals his vulnerability with lame excuses ("Outragedy of poetscalds! Acomedy of letters! I have them all, tame, deep and harried, in my mine's I" [425.24]) and evasion of the issue ("I would never for anything take so much trouble of such doing" [425.33]). Shaun hates Shem for his "root language" (424.17) with good reason: at the end of the Justice and Mercy debate Shaun "points the deathbone and the quick are still" (193.29), while Shem "lifts the lifewand and the dumb speak" (195.5).[17] Shaun as "our handsome young spiritual physician that was to be" (191.16) is defeated by "Pain the Shamman" (192.23)—calling to mind Lévi-Strauss's explanation that the shaman heals by providing the patient with a language.[18]

Many infantile traumas inform the anxieties that rule the dream world of *Finnegans Wake*. The infant's sense of powerlessness pervades many Wakean fantasies: the child's bewilderment and exclusion in viewing the parental sex act, the jealous love for the parent of the opposite sex, the trial of acquiring control over bodily functions, and the terror of feeling one's reality suspended between one's body and the mirror image. The many violent events in *Finnegans Wake* are plausible as expressions of infantile combat against this powerlessness: taking the mother away from the father, aggressive defecation and urination, stealing words with which to slander everyone, like young Stephen at boarding school feeling the mysterious power of "smugging," "suck," and "belt."

Finnegans Wake contains another configuration explicitly representing the *stade du miroir:* Isabel and her looking glass image. James Atherton finds the source of Isabel's split image in Morton Prince's account of a female split personality, whose two major components rival Shem and Shaun in antagonism and paranoia.[19] In contrast, Isabel's relationship to her alter ego, Maggie or Madge, is one of simple narcissism. The program at the Feenichts Playhouse lists Isabel as, "IZOD (Miss Butys Pott ...), a bewitching blonde who dimples delightfully and is approached in loveliness only by her grateful sister reflection in a mirror" (220.7). Joyce spares the women in his later works the self-contempt that afflicts his males, and their self-love is often expressed in their mirrors. Gerty MacDowell knows "how to cry nicely before the mirror. You are lovely, Gerty, it said" (*U*, p. 351). Molly Bloom likewise remembers her juvenile narcissism, "I used to love myself then stripped at the washstand dabbing and creaming" (*U*, p. 763).

Because of their narcissism, Joyce's women need not compete and war with one another for self-possession, as do their brothers. Hardly a feminist, even Molly Bloom speculates, "I dont care what anybody says itd be much better for the world to be governed by the women in it you wouldnt see women going and killing one another and slaughtering" (*U*, p. 778). But the lack of alienation and intrasubjective conflict costs the women a price in self-awareness. Asked about immortality, struggle for life, and Darwinism, Issy—like Gerty MacDowell—can only think of romance, sex, and simple piety ("Of I be leib in the immoralities? O, you mean the strangle for love and the sowiveall of the prettiest? Yep, we open hab coseries in the home" [145.26]). Only the women of the early works, Eveline, Gretta Conroy, and Bertha Rowan, suffer internal conflict and alienation—an alienation of the ego like that experienced in the *stade du miroir,* and which, according to Lacan, is a precondition for human knowledge.[20]

Like Gerty and Molly, Isabel is a temptress. But unlike the complex, mediated desires of men, the psychology of female desire is so narcissistic as to be primitive by Hegelian standards. In the monologues of Gerty, Molly, and Isabel, the men are virtually pretexts for fantasies about clothes, undergarments, perfumes, the accouterments of their own bodies, as though the women were their own erotic objects ("God I wouldnt mind being a man and get up on a lovely woman" [*U*, p. 770]). Yet by combining Isabel's role as a temptress with the mirror-image double, Joyce has utilized the narcissistic components of her characterization to create a further ingenious and subtle example of triangular desire in one of the major configurations of *Finnegans Wake:* the old man with two girl-loves.

The triangle's analogues, representing HCE's attraction to his divided daughter that brings about his fall in the Phoenix Park incident, include Swift-Stella-Vanessa, Daddy Browning and the peaches, and Napoleon-Josephine-Marie Louise. But it is the allusions to Charles Dodgson in *Finnegans Wake,* impressively enumerated and explained by James Atherton,[21] that most clearly contain both the theme of mirror-image narcissism and the old man-young girls configuration: Alice and her looking glass image ("Nircississies are as the doaters of inversion. Secilas through their laughing classes" [526.34]) and Dodgson's susceptibility to little girls, particularly Alice Liddle and Isa Bowman, "isabeaubel" (146.17). Freud explains in his essay on narcissism how the two configurations are related.

Such women have the greatest fascination for men, not only for aesthetic reasons, since as a rule they are the most beautiful, but also because of certain interesting psychological constellations. It seems very evident that one person's narcissism has a great attraction for those others who have renounced part of their own narcissism and are seeking after object-love; the charm of a child lies to a great extent in his narcissism, his self-sufficiency and inaccessibility. . . .[22]

Lewis Carroll's Alice is undoubtedly the charming, self-sufficient child *par excellence* in literature, and Carroll, like HCE, is a man who loves little girls because they love themselves.

Since the girl-child's self-love engenders the old man's desire for her, the configuration forms an attenuated situation of "triangular desire." In the Tristan myth, Joyce superimposes the conventional love triangle of the old man-woman-young man oedipal type with the figure of the old man and two girls: Iseult is a type of Isabel ("Iseult la belle" [398.29]), split into the doubles of Isolde of Brittany and Isolde of Ireland. The Tristan myth in *Finnegans Wake,* therefore, duplicates the sin in Phoenix Park to demonstrate intersecting incestuous desires: Isabel, combining functions of mother and daughter, is the object of both the father and the sons in their struggle for family primacy.

IN THE NAME OF THE FATHER

While the family in *Finnegans Wake* is a complicated psychological constellation, it also serves as the paradigm of a primal social structure.

The problem of relating the psychological and social significance of family dynamics is not without precedent: Freud himself delineated the social analogue of the Oedipus complex in *Totem and Taboo*. The investigation into the sin in Phoenix Park delves into life's most fundamental mysteries, the mystery of human origin, the mystery of sex fraught with the prohibited oedipal wishes. Yet while incest and parricide are crimes committed in the bosom of the family, they are of all crimes most worthy of public concern, since they strike at the very foundation of the social order. Oedipus's sins jeopardize society and must, therefore, be publicly tried and punished. HCE's family affairs, likewise, become the leaven of a veritable "hubbub caused in Edenborough" (29.36).

Joyce discovered and utilized a third theory of social origins to complement his use of the Edenic and Oedipus myths in *Finnegans Wake*. Found in Vico's *Scienza Nuova*, this myth significantly juxtaposes the origins of society and language. The following translator's summary retells Vico's account of the event when the sky first thundered.

The descendants of Ham and Japheth and the non-Hebraic descendants of Shem, having wandered through the great forest of the earth for a century or two, had lost all human speech and institutions and had been reduced to bestiality, copulating at sight and inclination. These dumb beasts naturally took the thundering sky to be a great animated body, whose flashes and claps were commands, telling them what they had to do. The thunder surprised some of them in the act of copulation and frightened copulating pairs into nearby caves. This was the beginning of matrimony and of settled life.[23]

Vico's myth skillfully illustrates the impossibility of civilized society amid conditions of sexual promiscuity and mutism. Vico's postdiluvial peoples specifically lack a law-governed system of exchange, which would establish order and communication among them. Kinship laws are therefore a major prerequisite for civilization. "The primordial Law is therefore that which in regulating marriage ties superimposes the kingdom of culture on that of nature abandoned to the law of copulation."[24] Kinship laws, such as the incest taboo, govern a system of possible combinations in mating, and are therefore analogous to linguistic laws, such as phonotactic laws which govern the possible combinations of sounds, and syntactic laws which govern the combination of words in a sentence. "This law, therefore, (the incest prohibition) is revealed clearly enough as identical to an order of Language. For without kinship nominations, no power is capable of instituting the order of preferences and taboos which bind and weave the yarn of lineage down through succeeding generations."[25]

Both kinship systems and language, instituted by the clap of thunder in Vico's myth, serve the foundation of civilization by introducing those dintinctions that linguistically and socially constitute meaningful systems. The source of this meaning in the myth is the voice of the thunder, which in Eliot's *Wasteland* spoke its humanizing commands, and which, interpreted as the voice of God by "the dumb beasts," functions as a version of the theological Word or Logos.

Although Joyce clearly derived the thunder in *Finnegans Wake* from Vico, the image is as polyvalent and overdetermined as all other elements in the dream. Its significance is concealed not only in the hundred letters of its name, but also in the contexts and associations that surround it. The thunder is associated with male conflict, presumably the father's fall, "the hundering blundering dunderfunder of plundersundered manhood" (596.2). It is always sounded at moments of great crisis, like the Prankquean's assault, the publication of the scurrilous ballad or the letter, the trials of HCE in the tavern and of Shaun on the mound, and the father's interruption of the children's sexual play, like Vico's thunder or the fireworks on Sandymount Strand in "Nausicaa."

Because the thunder occurs when the father is falling, it is analogous to other noises that suggest sin or guilt in the work. These are human noises, like HCE's stutter that itself resembles the garbled speech of Tom Kernan, who in "Grace" fell drunkenly down the pub's WC steps and bit off a corner of his tongue. The thunder also resembles the thumping, bumping noise of someone falling down a ladder," . . . drumstrumtruminahumptadump . . . "(314.8), or the noise of a shutter being shut after HCE is threatened by the Prankquean and later by a lynch mob outside his tavern, or when the father shuts the door in several languages after bringing the children in for the night, "Lukkedoerendunandurraskewdylooshoofermoyporter . . . " (257.27). The thunder is a cough that interrupts Shaun while telling his fable. It is also, of course, the anal/gunshot noises of the father shitting or being shot.

It is difficult to determine the common link of all these manifestations of the thunder, unless it is the klang-association of thunder-shutter-stutter-shitter-shooter, a connection not at all unlikely in a dream-work since the unconscious connects words by sounds as well as meaning. It is clear, in any event, that all of these activities suggest either Wakean sins, like shitting and shooting, or guilt, like stuttering, nervous coughing, or shutting oneself away from persecution. *Wake* thunder, unlike Vico's thunder, does not function as the civilizing command of God. On the contrary, instead of promoting matrimony, the thunder words themselves express obscenities ("... foul ... whor ... strump ... porn ... kocks ... tupper ... strip ..." [90.31]). James Atherton coalesces thunder and stutter as symptom of the original sin of God, "Joyce is suggesting that the original masterbuilder is God and that He stutters when his voice is heard in the thunder—thus proving that He is conscious of having committed a sin!"[26]

As Vico's thundering God is law-giver, so the *Wake*'s thundering HCE is law-breaker. If the thunder is understood as a language, either as authoritative or fallen, the father's symbolic function emerges more clearly. The Christian tradition defines the source of authority as the Word. The authority of the Symbolic father resides, therefore, in his name, because he names himself, designates his own function, and creates his own identity. Jacques Lacan writes, "It is in the *name of the father* that we must recognize the support of the Symbolic function which, from the dawn of history, has identified his person with the figure of the law."[27] The prototype of the Symbolic father is therefore the Mosaic God, whose justification as the source of law resides in the tautology of his name, the inviolable certainty of his identity. The Symbolic father, "he who is ultimately capable of saying 'I am who I am' "[28] is the center or pivot who defines, names, and gives meaning to the constellation of personages around him. *Finnegans Wake* contains numerous references to the Yahwistic "I am," as well as to the naming ritual of baptism, by means of the recurrent verbal motifs "mishe mishe" and "tauf tauf."[29]

The father corresponds to the semantic function of language; he is, as it were, the legal "equivalent to the law of speech which fixes each in his place."[30] The peculiar language of *Finnegans Wake* expresses the analogy between the law of man and the law of language. Broken language reveals the broken law, as Joyce may have learned from Freud's "The Psychopathology of Everyday Life," or from the accidents of history itself: the *Wake* contains frequent allusions to the misspelling of "hesitancy," which revealed Pigott's forgery at the Parnell inquiry.[31]

In *Finnegans Wake,* then, the Viconian myth of social and linguistic origin is essentially reversed: in Vico, the thunder creates language and kinship laws while in the *Wake,* the stutter serves as a symptom of linguistic breakdown and incestuous wishes. Edmund Epstein comments on the characteristic behavior of HCE as "nervous, stuttering denials that he ever thought of incest with his daughter alternate with fearful praise of his wife. . . ."[32] But denials are of no avail. During one of his trials he is charged with "Begetting a wife which begame his niece" (373.26); during a later inquest, irrepressible voices call out, "Rape the daughter! Choke the pope!" (500.17). An account of the Earwicker parents' copulation is interrupted by the passage often cited as the most lurid in the work. It tells the fable of the polymorphous sexual depravity in the household of Honophrius, a type of HCE (III.4). Involving every character cluster in the *Wake*—even those agents of inquiry and judgment, the four old men and the twelve customers of the pub—the story is a lively fantasy of incest ("Honophrius, Felicia, Eugenius and Jeremias are consanguineous to the lowest degree" [572.25]). Presented in the form of a case at law, these unseemly familial gambollings are claimed to be widespread, even universal, occurrences ("This, lay readers and gentilemen, is perhaps the commonest of all cases arising out of umbrella history . . . in our courts of litigation" [573.35]). "The incest that rules Earwicker's night ruled Freud's days," writes William York Tindall.[33]

The social consequence of incest is the destruction of the social order. Vico describes the underworld as the place where "vagrants remained in their infamous promiscuity. The god of this underworld is Erebus, called the son of Chaos; that is, of the confusion of human seeds."[34] Incest obliterates those distinctions that create a system of relationships in which every individual has a function and an identity. Laius's attempted infanticide robs the child Oedipus of his true identity and casts him among strangers. At the fatal crossroads father and son meet as strangers, an alienation consequent to Laius's disturbance of kinship laws—his "underestimation" of the father-son relationship, to borrow a term from Lévi-Strauss.

The great encounter between HCE and the cad in *Finnegans Wake* also involves mistaken identity and lack of recognition. HCE's clothes, as in all later accounts of this incident, comprise an eclectic foreign costume with India rubber military cap ("caoutchouc kepi" [35.8]), Indian gaiters ("Bhagafat gaiters" [35.10] also Bhagavad Gita), Scottish rain cape ("inverness" [35.10]), and a roadstaff reminiscent of Laius's two-pointed goad. The foreign, military costume suggests an analogue to native-invader confrontations in the *Wake*. The cad is carrying his overcoat ("overgoat" [35.13]) under his shoulder ("schulder" [35.13]: German, Schuld, sin, guilt) sheepside out, to look more like a comfortable, countrified gentleman. The allusion to the Jacob and Esau myth in this passage is important because it introduces into the HCE-cad encounter a cluster of provocative references to confused identity and unlawful family descent. The coat worn sheepside out to look more like the hirsute, country-boy Esau is, of course, the ploy used by Jacob to impersonate his brother and so defraud him of his lawful birthright. This also makes the cad something of a wolf in sheep's clothing, a further clue that all is not well and that HCE is right to be suspicious and defensive.

Interference with kinship laws causes the social fabric to unravel and identities to become indeterminate once again. When Oedipus discovers the truth of his double crime, he also learns his identity at last. But that identity is no more: as husband/son/father/brother there is no longer a locus in his relationships in which he might find definition. Like Oedipus, HCE is guilty of an ancient crime ("ages and ages after the alleged misdemeanour" [35.5]) that seems to involve the confusing of races and lineages consequent to violation of kinship laws ("the anniversary, as it fell out, of his first assumption of his mirthday suit and rights in appurtenance to the confusioning of human races" [35.3]). Pursuit of the criminal leads even deeper into the morass of his uncertain identity. "Whence it is a slopperish matter, given the wet and low visibility (since in this scherzarade of one's thousand one nightinesses that sword of certainty which would identifide the body never falls) to idendifine the individuone" (51.3).

This matter of the uncertainty and indeterminability of HCE's identity deserves special consideration because it is too easily dismissed as merely an aspect of his archetypal function, his embodiment of multitudes and subsequent lack of individuality. While all the Wakean characters have many names and conditions, these are not generally in themselves the subject of dispute in the narrative. Yet HCE's name and identity are the topic of frequent controversy. The uncertainty of HCE's identity must be accorded thematic rather than purely stylistic status in the work, since parricide and questions of identity are thematically related. In other words, questions of who HCE is and what he has done are inseparable.

Frequently, HCE is portrayed as everyman and no man. He is seen as "an imposing everybody he always indeed looked, constantly the same as and equal to himself and magnificently well worthy of any and all such universalisation" (32.19). He is called "a manyfeast munificent more mob than man" (261.21). However, the investigation into the HCE-cad encounter is thwarted by the retort, "But how transparingly nontrue, gentlewriter! His feet one is not a tall man, not at all, man. No such parson. No such fender. No such lumber. No such race" (63.9), and after a recount of his sins, he is warned, "First you were Nomad, next you were Namar, now you're Numah and it's soon you'll be Nomon" (374.22).

Like the father, the figure of law and authority, and namer of family members, the name of the father has special significance. His given name is uncertain from the start ("concerning the genesis of Harold or Humphrey Chimpden's occupational agnomen" [30.2]), he is even called "Haromphreyld" (31.8) to signify this initial confusion. The story of the origin of his surname is unconfirmed ("Comes the question are these the facts of his nominigentilisation as recorded and accolated in both or either of the collateral andrewpaulmurphyc narratives" [31.33]). It is by the presence of his initials in arbitrary three-word sequences, "tristurned initials, the cluekey to a worldroom beyond the roomwhorld" (100.28), that HCE is identified in most passages of the *Wake.* The initials are indeed merely a "cluekey" (clew: ball of thread used in guiding one's way out of a labyrinth), or a guideline through the maze of the *Wake.* In such sequences as "*H*aveyou-*c*aught-*e*merod's" (63.18),* "*h*ears *c*ricket on the *e*arth" (138.26), "*H*einz *c*ans every-where" (581.5), or the transposed "*c*oal at the *e*nd of his *h*arrow" (127.8), the initials tell us not *who* HCE is, but merely *where* he is present. Considered in the light of dream language, the initials signal a repressed reference to the father, an involuntary and unrecognized thought of him. We find the greatest multiplicity of HCE's names in the passage preceding "The Ballad of Persse O'Reilly," where he is named at will by the citizenry. "Some vote him Vike, some mote him Mike, some dub him Llyn and Phin while others hail him Lug Bug Dan Lop, Lex, Lax, Gunne or Guinn. Some apt him Arth, some bapt him Barth, Coll, Noll, Soll, Will, Weel, Wall but I parse him Persse O' Reilly else he's called no name at all" (44.10).[35]

*Italics mine.

In contrast to that certainty of identity which makes the Symbolic father the figure of the Law, the *Wake*'s father figure emerges as indeterminable, dependent, and variable by name. He is called "Cloudy father! Unsure! Nongood!" (500.18); and he resides, via initials, in the phrase "*Haud certo ergo*" (263.28), "nothing certain, therefore."

Leopold Bloom, the father in *Ulysses,* also has variable names since his family name has been changed from Virag to Bloom, and he uses "Flower" as a pseudonym in his guilty correspondence. Joyce's cynical notions of fatherhood, which Stephen calls a "necessary evil" and a "legal fiction," are amplified to primal and mythic proportions in the portrayal of HCE. "Fatherhood, in the sense of conscious begetting, is unknown to man. It is a mystical estate, an apostolic succession, from only begetter to only begotten. On that mystery and not on the madonna which the cunning Italian intellect flung to the mob of Europe the church is founded and founded irremovably because founded, like the world, macro- and microcosm, upon the void. Upon incertitude, upon unlikelihood" (*U,* p. 207). The very certitude of the name of the Mosaic God is challenged, then, as in the prophecy of Shaun ("you sprout all your abel and woof your wings dead certain however of neuthing whatever to aye forever while Hyam Hyam's in the chair" [455.21]). HCE as God in the *Wake* is invoked as "Ouhr Former who erred in having" (530.36). The paired Celtic-German refrain from the first page of the work—"mishe mishe": "I am, I am" and "tauf-tauf": "baptize, baptize"—is linguistically profaned throughout the work.

The Wakean vision of a universe ever hurtling toward chaos is based on the theme of the fallen father. He is named rather than namer. He is uncertain of name and identity, unlocatable rather than a center that fixes, defines, and gives meaning to his cosmos. He is a lawbreaker rather than lawgiver. As head of the family, he is incestuous rather than the source of order in the relations of his lineage.

REDEMPTION: THE FAILURE OF THE SON

From the orderly progression of Vico's downward spiral (theocracy-monarchy-democracy-anarchy) as well as from mythic and Freudian sources, we might expect the sons to assume the position of law and authority upon their parricide of the father. Freud says of the parricidal sons in *Totem and Taboo,* "They revoked their deed by forbidding the killing of the totem, the substitute for their father; and they renounced its fruits by resigning their claim to the women who had now been set free. They thus created out of their filial sense of guilt the two fundamental taboos of totemism, which for that very reason inevitably corresponded to the two̱ repressed wishes of the Oedipus complex."[36] The murder of the father, therefore, establishes a debt and a guilt that bind the son to the Law for life.[37]

The sons of HCE, however, appear to find no such redemption in the *Wake*. If Christ atoned for the sin of Adam and founded a spiritual kingdom on earth, Shaun in his reenactment of the *via crucis* and its commemorative, the Mass, perverts the salvation process and affirms a hypostatic union of shame with the Father and the Holy Ghost.

—Ouer Tad, Hellig Babbau, whom certayn orbits assertant re humeplace of Chivitas Ei, Smithwick, Rhonnda, Kaledon, Salem (Mass), Childers, Argos and Duthless. Well, I am advised he might in a sense be both nevertheless, every at man like myself, suffix it to say, Abrahamsk and Brookbear! By him it was done bapka, by me it was gone into, to whom it will beblive, Mushame, Mushame! (481.20).

In parody of the Lord's prayer, "Ouer Tad" is not so easily and centrally located in heaven (Chivitas Ei, civitas dei: state of god); he may also be found in Scotland, Greece, and Salem, Massachusetts. He is both patriarch (hellig, hellish, heilig: German, holy; Babbo: Italian, endearment for father; Abraham) and totem animal (Babbau, baboon, Brookbear)—"Well, I am advised he might in a sense be both nevertheless." He is also a terrifying figure of power and law as "tiptip tim oldy faher now the man I go in fear of" (481.31) (Babau: "bogie with which nurses in Languedoc terrify unruly children," according to Adaline Glasheen[38]). But the father and son are bound by a crime so great that even the self-name of the Mosaic God, "mishe mishe"—I am, I am— becomes "Mushame."

The precise nature of the criminal union of father and son adds a startling sexual dimension to the theme of parricide. In a veiled but interesting allusion to *Ulysses*, the three grenadiers or soldiers who surprise and attack the father throughout the *Wake* are described as a profane Trinity in III.3:

Three in one, one and three.
Shem and Shaun and the shame that sunders em.
Wisdom's son, folly's brother. (526.13)

The words "the shame that sunders em" recall Stephen's discussion of father-son incest in *Ulysses*. "They are sundered by a bodily shame so steadfast that the criminal annals of the world, stained with all other incests and bestialities, hardly record its breach. Sons with mothers, sires with daughters, lesbic sisters, loves that dare not speak their name, nephews with grandmothers, jailbirds with keyholes, queens with prize bulls" (*U*, p. 207).

In *Finnegans Wake* the sons are charged with violating this taboo of taboos, male homosexual incest—specifically buggery. The guilty fusiliers in "The Ballad of Persse O'Reilly" are the three soldier/sons who rise up against the father during the incident in Phoenix Park:

He was joulting by Wellinton's monument
Our rotorious hippopopotamuns
When some bugger let down the backtrap of the omnibus
And he caught his death of fusiliers, . . . (47.7)

During Shaun's inquest he is asked, "Did any orangepeelers or green-goaters appear periodically up your sylvan family tree?" (522.16). He answers with a revealing denial, "Buggered if I know!" (522.18), whereupon he is charged with "homosexual catheis of empathy between narcissism of the expert and steatopygic invertedness" (522.30).

In the manner of dreams, a number of closely related themes are superimposed or condensed in *Finnegans Wake* and thereby elaborated into a fabric of highly integrated psychic stuff. The most explicit instance of parricide in *Finnegans Wake* is Buckley's shooting of the Russian General, presented through the Butt and Taff skit in II.3. Buckley shoots the Russian General in the ass, after he has defecated and wiped himself with a bit of Irish sod. Like every story in the *Wake*, this one has its versions, including the Russian General impaled on a bishop's crozier ("I gave one dobblenotch and I ups with my crozzier. Mirrdo!" [353.19]), or shot with an arrow like Cock Robin ("With my how on armer and hits leg an arrow cockshock rockrogn. Sparro!" [353.20]). The sons' buggery and parricide of the father are, therefore, erotic/aggressive versions of the same act, the same sin, that is, the father's anal impalement.[39]

The father's sin, his defecation, is simply the reverse of the same act. So is Shaun's redemptive (Last Supper) activity in III.1. After an extravagant meal of "spadefuls of mounded food" (405.30), Shaun follows this Last Supper with the fourteen answers of his *via crucis* before catapulting into the Liffey in his barrel, in a kind of parody of Christ's ascension. This same disappearing act is so scatological as to thoroughly profane the sacred event of Christ's ascension. The narrator of the passage calls himself "I, poor ass" (405.6); and Shaun himself becomes "the soft semplgawn slob of the world" (426.10), a soft, foolish person, but also a soft lump in Gaelic. After a bit of sentimental weeping, he takes "a wipe at his pudgies" (426.14)–cheeks, we assume, reminding us of the Russian General who uses a bit of Irish sod for the purpose. Sleepily, Shaun looks at the star-studded heaven, when "the dreamskhwindel necklassoed him" (426.27) ("dreamskhwindel": Scandinavian, dreamy whorl or spiral; "windel": German, diaper) and caused him to lose the balance of "his ballbearing extremities" (426.29), which in a scatological passage are probably not feet. Dream reversal causes Shaun to descend rather than ascend. The dreamy spiral that lassoes Shaun suggests a stream of urine or the flush of a toilet,[40] as it causes Shaun's barrel to roll backwards into "Killesther's lapes and falls, with corks, staves and treeleaves and more bubbles" (427.1) until he is momentarily uprighted down in the valley "in a dip of the downs" (427.6), where he disappears and vanishes "like a popo (German: ass) down a papa, from circular circulatio" (427.7). There follows a gurgling "Gaogaogaone" (427.9) until only a single clue betrays his late presence, or the presence of his spirit, "A reek was waft on the luftstream. He was ours, all fragrance" (427.11).

Sin and redemption in terms of anal ingress and egress in the *Wake* reveal the failure of the father-son relationship to effect the stability of the social order through the restorative power of the Law. Redemption in *Finnegans Wake* does not result from the new covenant forged by the guilt of the sons, nor from a divine pardon. As in Christian mythology, redemption comes from a type of grace, but here a grace that transforms chaos into play, the loss of identity into freedom, and the fall of man into a celebration.

REDEMPTION: MATERNAL SALVAGE

The agent of grace and redemption in *Finnegans Wake* is Anna Livia Plurabelle, the mother of the Earwicker family and the river Liffey. Like male characters in the work, ALP is identified with all female characters; she therefore serves a dual role in relation to HCE as both temptress and savior. Although the function of the temptress as mediated object in the conflicts between fathers and sons has been discussed earlier, some reference to the means and motives of seduction will be necessary in order to examine ALP's redemptive role.

ALP attempts to rescue HCE from the persecution of the populace and to restore him to the position of the potent father.

> She who shuttered him after his fall and waked him widowt sparing and gave him keen and made him able and held adazillahs to each arche of his noes, she who will not rast her from her running to seek him till, with the help of the okeamic, some such time that she shall have been after hiding the crumbends of his enormousness in the areyou lookingfor Pearlfar sea, (ur, uri, uria!) stood forth ... with pawns, prelates and pookas pelotting in her piecebag, for Handiman the Chomp, Esquoro, biskbask, to crush the slander's head. (102.1)

ALP, crushing the slander's head, recalls the icon of Mary, crushing the head of the Edenic serpent. But ALP is as much a profane Mary as her son Shaun is a profane Christ. Unlike the immaculately conceived Virgin, ALP, already tainted in her youthful role as the temptress Eve, undertakes her mission of salvation burdened by "the weight of old fletch" (621.33), a scavenger woman collecting rubbish, or the muddy Liffey bearing Dublin's sewage out to sea.

ALP's redemptive act, like the sin in Phoenix Park, is retold in alternate versions of the same tale. In one, she is the scavenging old "turfwoman," (12.11) or a "gnarlybird ygathering" (10.32), distributing gifts and food; in another, she is the hen who scratches the letter from the dump or the faithful wife ("who but Crippled-with-Children would speak up for Dropping-with-Sweat?" [102.29]) delivering her "mamafesta" (104.4) to save her fallen man. Woman and hen are the same figure, and the letter and gifts of debris are analogues. The same actions characterize each of ALP's redemptive acts: finding and giving, gathering and dispersing. Her acts are not acts of atonement; "she is mercenary" (12.6), we are told. In *Finnegans Wake* the act of redemption is secular, not religious, an act of salvage rather than salvation.

ALP's scavenging and distribution of goods supports those functions upon which the viability of society depends: communication and exchange. Her actions can best be perceived as means of reconciliation, in contrast to the many unlawful appropriations in the work which sunder family members in divisive power struggles. According to Lévi-Strauss, communication in a society involves the exchange of women, goods and services, and messages; all three are the subject of culpable transactions in the *Wake*. There are shady financial dealings in the work, found in their most primitive form in the dialogue of Mutt and Jute, where a wooden nickel changes hands ("Let me fore all your hasitancy cross your qualm with trink gilt. Here have sylvan coyne, a piece of oak" [16.29]). Besides its probable worthlessness, the coin is a bribe, for "hesitancy" is a catch-word for lying in the *Wake*.[41] The pair who "excheck a few strong verbs weak oach eather" (16.8) presumably deal in faithless messages as well, reminding us of the word-stealing and counter-charges of lying about word-stealing in the brother conflict.

Other notable instances of stealing occur in the parallel but inverse tales of the Prankquean and the Norwegian captain ("Stop deef stop come back to my earin stop" [21.23] cries Jarl van Hoother, and later the ship's husband cries, "Stolp, tief, stolp, come bag to Moy Eireann!" [312.1]). ALP is the culprit only in the tale of the Prankquean, but in both tales the stealing of children, suit, dinner, and the like, serves the ultimate function of founding and uniting the family. The Prankquean's tricks and deceit are needed to civilize the fierce father. The Prankquean washes and converts the twins before returning them, and the Norwegian Captain is "popetithes" (326.6) before the wedding. ALP converts the heathen, and as Grace O'Malley and the stolen Irish bride, assimilates the Scandinavian (van Hoother and Norwegian Captain) into the Irish culture. She domesticates the rover ("His loudship was converted to a landshop" [332.23]), and they drink tea ("they all drank free" [23.7]) and produce babies ("he put off the ketyl and they made three" [332.2]). Like the Prankquean, the scavenging old ALP is a thief of sorts, ("where in thunder did she plunder" [209.12]), but her stealing is not for herself as she forever disperses her booty to her children ("How bootifull and how truetowife of her, when strengly forebidden, to steal our historic presents from the past postpropheticals so as to will make us all lordy heirs and ladymaidesses of a pretty nice kettle of fruit" [11.29]).

The unlawful appropriation of women, whether the bridestealing cuckoldry of the Tristan and Finn MacCool myths, or the incestuous fantasies that they represent, stands in significant contrast to ALP's efforts to procure women for her husband ("Calling them in, one by one . . . and legging a jig or so on the sihl to show them how to shake their benders. . . and all the way of a maid with a man . . . Throwing all the neiss little whores in the world at him!" [200.22]). The aim of her pandering is to restore HCE's potency, therefore aligning it with her distribution of food, gifts, and the Letter in an effort to reverse HCE's downfall.

ALP's acts are essentially selfless. She steals van Hoother's children, but returns them improved and at peace. She plunders the battlefield and the dump, but uses the junk and the Letter to bring about the reconciliation and restoration of others. ALP's work stands in opposition to the unlawful appropriations of father and sons because she does not seek self-possession through the capture of the other. The problem of ALP's own self is not posed until her final monologue, when she reclaims it by a total repudiation of all others.

The raw material of ALP's redemption is the debris and litter that results from battle, catastrophe, and destruction ("all spoiled goods go into her nabsack: curtrages and rattlin buttins . . . keys and woodpiles of haypennies and moonled brooches with bloodstaned breeks in em, boaston nightgarters and masses of shoesets and nickelly nacks and foder allmicheal and a lugly parson of cates and howitzer muchears" [11.18]). This grim military rubble she transforms into Christmas gifts which effect a kind of Christmas armistice perhaps best remembered in the nostalgic annals of World War I ("But it's the armitides toonigh, militopucos, and toomourn we wish for a muddy kissmans to the minutia workers and there's to be a gorgeups truce for happinest childher everwere" [11.13]). She appears on the scene after the biblical deluge that destroyed the world, as a "peacefugel" (11.9), a Noah's dove bearing the olive branch. The debris she gathers includes the scattered remains of her dismembered husband. Like Isis restoring her brother/husband (Osiris) to life, she manages to put Humpty Dumpty together again, and prepare him for communionlike distribution ("And even if Humpty shell fall frumpty times as awkward again in the beardsboosoloom of all our grand remonstrancers there'll be iggs for the brekkers come to mournhim, sunny side up with care" [12.12]). ALP as the faithful old wife also gathers together the shreds of HCE's reputation in the form of the "mamafesta" (104.4) she delivers, or the Letter the hen scratches from the dump. The Boston nightletter is one of the pieces of trash in ALP's litterbag ("boaston nightgarters and masses of shoesets" [11.22]), that serves as a redemptive gift ("Hen trieved it and plight pledged peace" [94.7]).

As the verbal motif of the "Felix culpa" announces throughout the work, ALP's redemptive act, like Christ's, requires a fall. Of the war, destruction, and catastrophe in the *Wake*, Marcel Brion writes in *Our Exagmination*, "This chaos is the condition necessary to all creation."[42] The interdependence of creation and destruction provides a further technical and thematic application of Bruno's contraries in *Finnegans Wake*.

The redemption/creation process itself, however, deserves careful study, beginning with some skepticism toward Brion's further analysis. "In this apparent chaos we are conscious of a creative purpose, constructive and architectural, which has razed every conventional dimension, concept and vocabulary, and selected from their scattered material the elements of a new structure."[43] ALP's distribution is an act of communication and exchange, rather than an act of reconstruction or design. She selects bits of rubble randomly; the nature of her gifts is arbitrary, and her mode of distribution, indiscriminate.[44] Her generosity respects no hierarchies, ranks, orders, or distinctions ("a cough and a rattle and wildrose cheeks for poor Piccolina Petite MacFarlane; a jigsaw puzzle of needles and pins and blankets and shins between them for Isabel, Jezebel and Llewelyn Mmarriage; a brazen nose and pigiron mittens for Johnny Walker Beg; a papar flag of the saints and stripes for Kevineen O'Dea; a puffpuff for Pudge Craig and a nightmarching hare for Techertim Tombigby" [210.9]). If law is a structuring, ordering principle governing societal systems, then ALP's gift-giving is unsystematic and anarchic. She observes no such distinctions as those that lie at the foundation of the concept of law, which is based on the orders of preference, and on prohibitions, as is language itself.

The fact that ALP's gifts are trivial or nonsensical does not diminish their value as tokens of good will and gestures of peace. ALP even unites her enemy sons for a time ("like Santa Claus at the cree of the pale and puny, nistling to hear for their tiny hearties, her arms encircling Isolabella, then running with reconciled Romas and Reims, on like a lech to be off like a dart, then bathing Dirty Hans' spatters with spittle, with a Christmas box apiece for aisch and iveryone of her childer" [209.23]). Jacques Lacan explains that gifts are symbols and symbols are pacts. The uselessness and superfluity of gifts is proof of their symbolic value.[45]

As Dionysius, Osiris, and Christ are mythical analogues of the sacrificial god, so ALP's redemptive act occurs in several analogous forms: the gathering of junk and distribution of gifts, the retrieval of the Letter from the midden heap and its presentation to save HCE, and, quite likely, Joyce's production of *Finnegans Wake* itself. The linguistic correspondence of ALP's gathering is etymologically valid according to philosopher Martin Heidegger. "Originally *logos* did not mean speech, discourse. Its fundamental meaning stands in no direct relation to language. *Legó, legein,* Latin *legere,* is the same as the German word "lesen" (to gather, collect, read) . . . "ein Buch lesen" (to read a book) is only a variant of "lesen" in the strict sense, which is: to put one thing with another, to bring together, in short, to gather; but at the same time the one is marked off against the other."[46]

Certainly the process of reading *Finnegans Wake*—or the hen's Letter, insofar as we see the text—represents a primitive sort of *lesen:* not the rapid, automatic decoding to which we are accustomed, but a slow, patient, bringing together, putting one thing with another, looking for similarities and contrasts rather than intrinsic meanings.

That Joyce was not only aware of the etymological information just cited, but also deemed it relevant to *Finnegans Wake,* is demonstrated by Beckett's description of the evolution of the Latin word "Lex," found in his essay in *Our Exagmination.*

1. Lex = Crop of acorns
2. Ilex = Tree that produces acorns
3. Legere = To gather
4. Aquilex = He that gathers the waters
5. Lex = Gathering together of peoples, public assembly
6. Lex = Law
7. Legere = To gather together letters into a word, to read[47]

The prototypical meaning of "Lex" as a gathering together of peoples sheds further light on ALP's success in peacemaking through her gathering and gift-giving. This earlier meaning of law does not yet contain reference to the authoritative and prohibitive aspects of law as we know it, aspects that relate the concept of law to the figure of the father. In contrast to the father, ALP, the mother, embodies the law as a lack. She does not arrange, regulate, designate, or judge, but merely gathers together her children and the fragments of her fallen husband. The linguistic correspondence of her function is the potentiality of language for an infinite number of combinations within a finite system, rather than the semantic function of language. ALP's law may be the law of the great maternal deities, who Freud believed "perhaps in general have preceded the father-gods."[48]

Neither ALP's redemptive efforts, nor the Letter, function as an atonement or a pardon in the tradition of Christian salvation. Nor do they serve an architectural function, the creation of a new society or the restoration of HCE's tattered reputation through a Letter of authoritative meaning. Instead, the Letter, like ALP's gifts, is a product of the fall itself, a tea-stained bit of litter from the dump whose content, as far as we can tell, consists of the flotsam and jetsam of family life and history: news, gossip, requests, and more accounts of the fall. The redemptive act in the *Wake* appears to be the acceptance and celebration of the fall rather than the institution of a new covenant, or the restoration of the Kingdom of God.

That the Letter is itself a further manifestation of the fall can be seen in its intriguing resemblence to HCE himself. Like HCE, its origins are obscure ("Say, baroun lousadoor, who in hallhagal wrote the durn thing anyhow?" [107.36]), and there exist a number of different accounts. One version has it that the Letter was originally sent from Boston, Massachusetts, possibly by someone named Maggy (111.9), who may also be the silent mirror reflection of Isabel. Other accounts suggest that the entire family had a hand in it ("Letter, carried of Shaun, son of Hek, written of Shem, brother of Shaun, uttered for ALP, mother of Shem, for Hek, father of Shaun" [420.17]). Again, like HCE and all other characters in the *Wake,* it has no true title and yet a multiplicity of names, "Her untitled mamafesta memorialising the Mosthighest has gone by many names at disjointed times" (104.4). The text of the Letter is as indeterminate as "the unmistaken identity of the persons in the Tiberiast duplex" (123.30) whose revelation is promised throughout the Letter and throughout the work, but never delivered. As with HCE's nature and actions, we receive a number of versions of the Letter's text: it deals variously with general family trivia ("well how are you Maggy & hopes soon to hear well" [111.16]); a list of ALP's desires, including a new bankside, love-making, gainful employment as a washerwoman, and a romp on the beach (201.5); gossip of the father's tribulations and a request for money (301.5); and a review of all the themes in the *Wake*, particularly the original sin business with a bias toward HCE's innocence (615.12). Atherton goes so far as to consider the Letter as "something crooked and depraved."[49] Tindall calls it "trivial, illiterate, and repetitious,"[50] not unlike ALP herself, who sings, babbles, fiddles, whistles, and crows throughout most of the chapter devoted to her.

Whatever the Letter may be, it is *not* a document that clarifies anything, proves anything, renders any verdict, or pardons anyone. We are no more certain about its origin, name, or meaning than we are of any other character or event in the work. If anything, its own slovenly condition and confusing content affirm and manifest the chaos of the fall. As just one among the "literrish fragments" (66.25) in ALP's womblike mail pouch, the Letter's value is not its message or its meaning, but—like her other tacky gifts—its function as a token of peace and reconciliation.

The legend of the Letter suggests that it not only affirms the condition of the fall, but also celebrates it. Paradoxically, it is said to be "sealed with crime" (94.8) yet "made ma make merry" (94.10). The same paradox informs the "felix culpa" motif and the "lots of fun at Finnegan's Wake" refrain, which broadcast throughout the work their boisterous and happy celebration of fatal tumbles and broken laws.

The grace that effects redemption in *Finnegans Wake* seems to be the triumph of freedom over law, a freedom expressed in every thematic ambiguity and uncertainty, every aberrant lexical item or syntactical distortion of the work.

It is ALP in her final monologue who accepts the passing of the generations, their blood commingled ("Yes, you're changing, son-husband, and you're turning, I can feel you, for a daughterwife from the hills again. . . . Try not to part! Be happy, dear ones!" [627.1]). In her final renunciation, she nonetheless acknowledges her former celebration of her husband ("I thought you the great in all things, in guilt and in glory" [627.23]). Musing upon the world founded on the void, upon incertitude and unlikelihood, Stephen comments, "*Amor matris*, subjective and objective genetive, may be the only true thing in life" (*U,* p. 207). "I done me best when I was let" (627.13), says ALP.

The most striking image of ALP as the agent of freedom through communication or exchange, and freedom's triumph over the law, is as Arrah-na-Pogue, from the play by Dion Boucicault.[51] Arrah, in the play, saves her foster brother from execution for his role in the political uprising, by a kiss, during which she effects an exchange from her mouth to his of a small scroll containing the plans for his escape. This richly symbolic vignette contains attenuated reference to both oedipal crimes, incest and parricide. Joyce amplifies the incestuous innuendoes of the chaste brother-sister kiss in "Arrah-na-pogue, in the otherworld of the passing of the key of Two-tongue Common" (385.3), where the reference to Tutenkamen recalls his famous brother-sister marriage. The parricide is implicit in the brother's leadership of a political rebellion, which recalls the instances of imperial conflict (Napoleon and Wellington, Buckley and the Russian General) as types of the father-overthrow in *Finnegans Wake*. But Arrah's letter, like ALP's, is the key to freedom—not pardon—but the triumph over the law. And as Atherton points out,[52] we find among ALP's last few words in the work, "Lps. The keys to. Given!" (628.15), which—though resonating against the New Testament's "Power of the Keys" by which the Son of God empowered man with his authority—will open not the kingdom of Heaven, but the free "chaosmos" that is *Finnegans Wake*.

4

THE ONTOLOGICAL CONDITION

GUILT

Joyce's fictional characters are always alienated from their worlds. In the paralyzed citizens of *Dubliners* and in Stephen's agitated defense against societal institutions in *Portrait,* the assault on the self is from without, and therefore defensible with silence, cunning, and exile, as Stephen concludes at the end of *Portrait.* Yet in Joyce's later works, the self becomes increasingly imperiled from within, as Stephen is gnawed by "agenbite of inwit," and Bloom tormented by sexual guilts in *Ulysses.* Joyce exquisitely balances the psychological and social processes of guilt in *Ulysses.* Bloom's alienation is simultaneously sexual and racial; as the Wandering Jew, subject to forbidden fantasies, he reflects an exiled Odysseus, driven and delayed by sexual desire. But Bloom most perfectly fuses the psychological and social functions of guilt in the mythic analogue of Christ, the divine masochist.

The fundamental difference between *Ulysses* and *Finnegans Wake* is greater than the difference between day and night. In *Ulysses,* the differences between inside and outside, self and other, individual and society, are still clearly delineated. Ulyssean characters have stable identities, notwithstanding their mythical analogues, and a consistent and unitary consciousness through which they largely know who they are and who everyone else is. But Wakean figures, as figures in a dream,

face the dilemma announced in a witty chapter title of Adaline Glasheen's *Second Census,* "Who's Who When Everybody is Somebody
Else." The gossips who publish the rann that destroys HCE's reputation
are figures of HCE himself, and of his sons. They sleep in drunken
stupor, like Treacle Tom who stutters "alcoh alcoho alcoherently"
(40.5) when dreaming of the temptresses—like HCE at the end of the
tavern sequence in II.3. Hosty is a complex figure, as Tindall points out,
sharing simultaneously the characteristics of patricidal son and filicidal
father.[1] He destroys HCE's reputation by publishing the rann, like
Shem "abusing his deceased ancestors" (173.20). But he is also like
HCE as paranoid father, who fears he may go mad either from too
much soul-searching ("selfabyss" [40.23]), or from self-abuse while
sitting on a wooden commode ("twoodstool" [40.23]), or from toad-
stool poisoning, perhaps administered by the night beerman ("birman"
[40.24]), whose drought may induce Danish night-madness.[2] While
unsuccessfully trying to gain admittance into various Dublin hospitals,
he dreams of avenging himself with "one sure shot bottle" (40.32),
whose context might be either drink or murder (bottle/battle). Since a
man can simultaneously be a father and a son, this duality of murderous roles, Laius and Oedipus, is a plausible phenomenon in the
dream. The lodging house from which the troupe of derelicts issues
forth to publish the rann, is called "The Barrel" (41.17), associating it
with Shaun, and making it analogous to another dwelling from which
nasty literature issues forth, Shem's house, "The Haunted Inkbottle,"
in I.7. Shaun is the barrel, as Shem is the squid-produced ink. Brothers,
houses, and artifacts therefore become literary and scatological versions
of one another as producers of nasty literature, or "shit." Such literary/
scatological production is culpable and therefore subject to control and
censure, as the infant learns at toilet training, and as Joyce learned
through censorship and obscenity trials. Guilt is one of the prime
movers in the dream world of *Finnegans Wake.* The theme of guilt in
Finnegans Wake, and the interchangeability of characters are related in
important ways. Interchangeability in the *Wake* is too easily dismissed
as a stylistic flourish, as an instance of the kind of typological cross-
identification found in Joyce's work as early as "Counterparts." Substitutions of personae, composite figures, disguises, and other instances of
shifting identity have important specific functions in the dream, as we
know from Freud's work, and as Joyce is certain to have known.
Besides gratifying the subject's wishes, the unconscious can simulta-

neously communicate and conceal unpleasant or painful matters by using various disguises. For example, the trivial action of uncorking a bottle is exalted as a religious rite in order to disguise its degrading scatological resonances ("pressures be to our hoary frother, the pop gave his sullen bulletaction and, bilge, sled a movement of catharic emulsipotion down the sloppery slide" [310.35]). The dream censor will be fooled by the papal blessing ("praises be to our Holy Father, the pope gave his solemn benediction, or papal bull, and led a movement of Catholic Emancipation"), from recognizing that the "catharic emulsi-potion" is the laxative that causes the pubkeeper to explosively soil his pants. This embarrassing situation prompts thoughts of a new suit of clothes, in the form of the tale of Kersse and the Norwegian Captain, and later, when HCE tries to find his other "courtin troopsers" (319.22) he finds that his porter has misplaced them "behind the oasthouse" (319.23). The sudden "bulletaction" of the explosive un-corking suggests that the papal bull may be merely bilge, or bullshit, as well as the sound of a shot—creating resonances of the shitting and shooting of the Russian General. HCE is not only a major figure in each episode, but he is also possibly both narrator and listener of the tales about himself. He is described as cupping his ear to catch the gossip of the customers in the pub; their "drohnings" (321.28) threaten to "drown" him in a Noah-like deluge, since his ear, a gigantic "meatous conch" (310.12) like that of a colossus, buzzes with the annoying roar of the insect- or earwig-like (Earwicker) customers. Insofar as personal pronouns are linguistic shifters, denoting senders, receivers, and topics of the message, HCE occupies all positions simultaneously, and is "I," "you," and "he" all at once. The dreamer, of course, is author, actor, and audience of his dream; he frequently, however, does not recognize himself there on the stage, and refuses to admit that he wrote the script.

The difficulty of distinguishing "self" and "other" makes the status of guilt extremely problematic in the *Wake*. Insofar as Wakean figures are often projections of themselves, the "other" can be regarded as the guilty self, and the characters' attitudes and comments toward others are often unconsciously self-reflexive. Joyce first suggests something of this sort in the description of Mr. Duffy in *Dubliners*. "He had an odd autobiographical habit which led him to compose in his mind from time to time a short sentence about himself containing a subject in the third person and a predicate in the past tense" (*D*, p. 108).

Joyce's sources for the technique of projecting guilt to trap a sinner undoubtedly include Shakespeare's "mousetrap" in *Hamlet*, and, perhaps, Oedipus's unwitting persecution of the murderer of Laius. In *Finnegans Wake*, HCE sympathetically joins the Russian General in a universal *mea culpa.* "We all, for whole men is lepers, have been nobbut wonterers in that chill childerness which is our true name after the allfaulters" (355.33). It is easier both to punish and forgive the fault of the "other" than of the self; ALP does so saying, "I will confess to his sins and blush me further" (494.30). However, at the merest suspicion that he himself might stand accused of a crime, HCE bursts into a hysterical, stuttering self-defense ("I protest there is luttrelly not one teaspoonspill of evidence at bottomlie to by babad" [534.9]).

Persecution is a major activity in *Finnegans Wake,* and its impetus is displaced guilt. The subject who has projected his guilt onto another can then wage a moral campaign against him, and therefore punish his own sin in the other. Shaun, as Justius, blatantly proposes a smear campaign ("We'll do a whisper drive, for if the barishnyas got a twitter of it they'd tell the housetops and then all Cadbury would go crackers" [193.13]) and ends up giving credence to his own gossip ("That a cross may crush me if I refuse to believe in it" [193.24]).

The question of guilt is insoluble in *Finnegans Wake* precisely because of its circularity. Seen from the perspective of the nursery, HCE is the aggressor in the Phoenix Park incident, frightening the children, exposing himself, exploiting their immaturity with sexual intimidation. But seen from the perspective of HCE as an impotent old man, the children are the aggressors. The sons, now young soldiers, threaten him with their virility, while the daughter tempts him with teasing exposure. Ultimately, neither father nor sons are spared persecution. Shem is forced into self-protective house arrest by a lynch mob, as is HCE, the publican. Shaun is harrassed into confession on the mound, as is HCE by the customers of his pub. Their persecutions are versions of one another, all of which Joyce has treated before in earlier works— the persecution of artists by priests, of priests by artists, of artists and priests by Philistine securlarists, and of Philistine secularists by artists and priests.

The psychological defense mechanism of projection has its social analogue in the scapegoat ritual. While the individual thrusts his personal guilt onto another, the society expels its collective guilt in the form of a sacrificial victim—the Greek pharmakos, the Hebraic scape-goat, the Christian Lamb of God. The process only works, however, if the individual or the society believe that the blame is truly transferred to an "other," who is not recognized as an objectified figure of the self. René Girard writes, "In the case of physical violence, the cure is genuine insofar as the community is truly re-unified against the single victim, inso-far, therefore, as the evil qualities of this random victim are unanimously and uncritically accepted."[3] Literature that explores the scapegoat ritual through the consciousness of the victim inevitably exposes the lie implicit in the process; it is only a matter of time before Hester Prynne's *A* becomes ubiquitous, appearing on Dimmesdale's chest, or, like a comet, in the sky to signify the community's guilt. Yet Hester is an acquiescent victim, as is Christ, who voluntarily assumes the sins of the world. As such a Christ figure, Shaun is a consummate failure in *Finnegans Wake*. He accepts as little guilt as possible ("meas minimas culpads!" [483.35]), blames others for the crimes investigated in the course of his "psychosinology," and pleads ignorance of the language when the going gets too rough ("Me no angly mo, me speakee Yell-man's lingas. . . . Me pigey savvy a singasong anothel time" [485.29]). Neither the processes of psychological projection nor social scape-goating succeed in removing guilt because there is no true distinction between self and other in the *Wake*. Shaun serves neither as malevolent "other" nor as passive victim. Like his father, he boasts of his solid respectability (his "patrician morning coat of arms" [485.1]), rails at his accusers ("Well, chunk your dimned chink" [484.15]), and even accuses his twin of being the scapegoat or "skipgod" (488.22). Accusers and accused, persecutors and victims all come to the same thing in the end: everyone is guilty and everyone denies it.

Wakean figures pursue the cause of guilt, the mysterious sin, as though searching for an apocalypse. Yet the sin, like the sinner, is universal in the end running the gamut of Freudian desires—involving bodily functions (urination, defecation), sexual longings (oral gratifica-tion, voyeurism, homosexual desires), and familial relationships (inces-tuous longings, aggression toward rivals). Everyone is guilty because everyone is human, born with a physical body from a mother and a father. This utterly fundamental source of guilt eludes Wakean figures as it eludes the psychoanalytic patient. The significance of guilt in *Finnegans Wake* lies not in the outcome of the quest for primal sin and sinner, but rather in the failure of the quest. It is repression, not sin, that is the more salient issue in the work. Wakean figures are ever searching for the fall, yet the fall is in their searching.

The problem of guilt in *Finnegans Wake* necessitates defining the reality, or level of reality, in the work. It is all too easy to treat Wakean figures as though they were characters in a nineteenth century novel, characters in fiction who mirror characters in life. But if we assume that *Finnegans Wake* represents a dream, then Wakean figures become the creatures of the dreamer, figures that may represent persons in an offscreen waking reality, or the dreamer himself, or a camouflage for others, or composites of several figures, like Freud's friend R and his uncle.[4] The great problem, of course, is that the reader is trapped inside the dream in *Finnegans Wake*. A dream can't be analyzed from the inside, because the dream is precisely the place where self-knowledge breaks down. The dreamer confronts a disguised message from his own unconscious. He is unable to know his unconscious directly, and yet it is utterly and truly himself. The confusion of the reader of *Finnegans Wake* is a fitting response to a kind of terror implicit in the world of the dream, a terror confronted by Alice in *Through the Looking-Glass* when Tweedledee suggests that she is merely a sort of thing in the Red Knight's dream.

The extent to which we can explore the problems of guilt and the self in psychoanalytic terms is limited by the absence of the frame of a waking reality in *Finnegans Wake*. In *Ulysses,* the fabulous distortions of "Circe" are fully intelligible in light of all we know of the day's events. The sources of the fantasy of Molly in Turkish costume (*U*, p. 439-41) are wonderfully diverse: Bloom's dream on the previous night; his thoughts of Agendath Netaim; serving Molly her breakfast in bed; his fear, pleasure, and shame at Molly's adultery; the scent of lemon soap in his pocket; and so on. But without the waking events and conscious thoughts of the subject, it is difficult to make sense of Wakean events in terms of the feelings and relations between individuals. Many of the issues raised in *Finnegans Wake,* like those in Carroll's books, are finally metaphysical rather than psychological or social. The subject of guilt in particular, is most profitably pursued as an ontological problem. In other words, events in *Finnegans Wake* elucidate the human condition, particularly the relationship of the self and other, in an abstract and timeless way, rather than in the concrete specific terms of the earlier works. The problem of guilt, the interchangeability of characters, the pursuit of truth, and the source of guilt through gossip and meandering talk, all of these issues conspire to represent a self utterly dislocated and lost. In exploring these issues, reference to the works of philosopher Martin Heidegger is particularly helpful, since Heidegger, like Joyce, is concerned with "everydayness." Moreover, Heidegger, in his contemporary concern with the relationship of the self to others, addresses himself to the ontological aspects of guilt in relation to the dislocated self.

IDLE TALK

"Dreams go by contraries" (U, p. 571), announces the prostitute Florry, sounding like Bruno of Nola, during the debauch in "Circe." In the dream world of *Finnegans Wake*, Florry's principle seems indeed to apply, for lies signal the truth, solemn pronouncements are inconsequential, trivial chatter is germane, and the most assiduous denials conceal the most sensitive secrets. The Famous Letter, which is supposed to establish HCE's innocence, tells us nothing directly, but a great deal inadvertantly. In its understandably poor condition after excavation from the midden heap, an expert examines it. He concludes that the Letter's envelope is important, extends this recommendation to a scholarly apologia of contextual criticism ("to concentrate solely on the literal sense or even the psychological content of any document to the sore neglect of the enveloping facts themselves circumstantiating it is just as hurtful to sound sense" [109.12]), and reinforces his point with an off-the-cuff analogy, which becomes increasingly risqué. The expert compares the Letter's envelope to a woman's garments ("capable of being stretched, filled out, if need or wish were, of having their surprisingly like coincidental parts separated, don't they now, for better survey by the deft hand of an expert, don't you know?" [109.27]). The Letter tells us nothing while the "expert's" lechery, suspiciously like self-righteous Shaun's, is revealed in a casual, digressive remark.

In every narrative line of *Finnegans Wake*, one sees the operation of the kind of cross-purpose manifest in the Letter's explication: an intention to create the impression of innocence, respectability, and authority betrayed by inadvertant, and seemingly accidental, signs of guilt. Wakean figures, in a sense, create for us a fictional representation of themselves, a "mythic text," in which they fervently believe.

Simultaneously, slips of the tongue, accidental double entendres, and unintended ambiguities expose the lie of the "mythic" self and reveal an authentic self that is essentially guilty. The writing of the "mythic text" of the self is graphically rendered by Shem the Penman, who with an ink produced "through the bowels of his misery . . . wrote over every square inch of the only foolscap available, his own body" (185.33). This mythic text obscures the authentic self like murky ink hiding the squid that produced it ("with each word that would not pass away the squidself which he had squirtscreened from the crystalline world waned chagreenold and doriangrayer in its dudhud" [186.6]). The paradox of an authentic and inauthentic self, unconscious and conscious, hidden and exposed to public view, is fittingly embodied in an allusion to Oscar Wilde's *The Picture of Dorian Gray*.[5] Shem's "mythic text," or the inky blur of the squid, are apt metaphors for the inauthentic self, resembling those of modern psychoanalysis—the blank, the lie, the censored chapter of individual history.[6]

In recognizing in Wakean talk an attempt to conceal, censor, and divert attention from a guilty self, a new light is shed on the extraordinary prolixity of Wakean narrative. The testimony at the trial of HCE deserves particular attention in this regard, because it represents a concerted effort to establish the facts and determine the truth. Yet the commentary veers off, with deadly inevitability, into trivialities, digressions, and qualifications, until the matter at hand is virtually lost.

The evidence given at the trial by the eye, ear, nose, and throat witness (86.32), for example, tells of the attack on two kings by one, Hyacinth O'Donnell. This information or "fact" is buried in a confusing narrative with many irrelevant digressions. We learn much about the witness's appearance, demeanor, and life style, that sheds little light on the testimony itself. "Talking extensively about something," writes Martin Heidegger, "covers it up and brings what is understood to a sham clarity—the unintelligibility of the trivial."[7] As always, this obfuscation in the *Wake* narrative seems motivated by guilt and fear. The significant undercurrent of the testimony, hidden in allusions and asides, is the dark theme of sexual, political, and religious heresies and persecutions.[8] The immense quantity of trivia, digression, and irrelevant matter interjected into the line of testimony betrays more guilt in its very defensiveness than do the actual accounts of the witnesses. In a sense, the rambling, peripheral style of much of the conversation in *Finnegans Wake* is the formal equivalent of HCE's guilty stutter.

The paradox of language is at the heart of the problem of guilt and the problem of the relationship of the self and the other. This paradox is simply the conflicting function of language as the instrument of man's simultaneous communication with and alienation from himself, others, and his world. Discourse has as its primary objective, communication and understanding, an understanding that, according to Heidegger, consists of grasping the entity being-talked-about in a primordial way. Yet this understanding becomes barred in *Gerede,* translated as "idle talk," by which Heidegger means not only gossip in the ordinary sense of the word, but all discourse that is unoriginal, a passing along of the thoughts and opinions of others, a use of dead expressions, worn-out idioms, clichés. "Because this discoursing has lost its primary relationship-of-Being towards the entity talked about, or else has never achieved such a relationship, it does not communicate in such a way as to let this entity be appropriated in a primordial manner, but communicates rather by following the route of *gossiping* and *passing the word along.* What is said-in-the-talk as such, spreads in wider circles and takes on an authoritative character. Things are so because one says so."[9]

In Joyce's work the gradual submersion in "idle talk" represents the paralysis of the citizenry that the artist must so vigorously resist if he is to preserve himself. Hugh Kenner notes Joyce's lifetime struggle with language, particularly its tropes, clichés, and the frozen language of the liturgy. "As a small boy James Joyce strained his imagination after secret connections between real things and the vocables his Dublin so prodigally disbursed. 'That was not a nice expression', P4/9; 'Suck was a queer word', P6/12; 'How could a woman be a tower of ivory or a house of gold?', P36/40."[10] Stephen's artistic evolution depends on his effort to pierce through ordinary usage in order to appropriate the entity-talked-about in a primordial manner. Yet Kenner points out in a citation from *Stephen Hero* how Stephen's original encounter with language is linked to a fascination with the speech of Dublin, the ordinary talk of its citizenry. "He read Skeat's *Etymological Dictionary* by the hour and his mind, which had from the first been only too submissive to the infant sense of wonder, was often hypnotized by the most commonplace conversation. People seemed to him strangely ignorant of the value of the words they used so glibly S26/20."[11]

A major difference between *Ulysses* and *Finnegans Wake* is the latter work's total submersion in idle talk. Stephen's cerebral musings on Sandymount Strand and Bloom's unflagging pseudo-scientific speculations are yet attempts at achieving a primordial grasp of one's world. But in *Finnegans Wake* the form and theme of every chapter is informed by a sham lust for knowledge, which degenerates all language into gossip, pedantry, tales, and slander. Sometimes the gossip is frankly acknowledged, as when the washerwomen qualify their tales of Anna Livia with "I heard he. . . . "(197.20); "I can't rightly rede you that. Close only knows. Some say she. . . . "(201.27); "Ay, you're right. I'm epte to forgetting" (208.4). Shaun, too, admits to a questionable assessment of his brother ("Putting truth and untruth together a shot may be made at what this hybrid actually was like to look at" [169.8]). More often, pompous official investigations disintegrate into blatant hearsay and storytelling ("But before proceeding to conclusively confute this begging question it would be far fitter for you, if you dare! to hasitate to consult with and consequentially attempt at my disposale of the same dime-cash problem elsewhere naturalistically of course, from the blinkpoint of so eminent a spatialist" [149.14]). Not only is the specialist evidently biased in the spatial-temporal controversy, but his presentation involves the questionable analogy of Roman history to butter, cheese, and margarine to account for sibling rivalry. In a work whose theme is the devastation of authority, the toppling of father/king, we observe the extent to which gossip about the father becomes authoritative. "The Ballad of Persse O'Reilly," which evolves from the baffling cad encounter through the circuits of the confessional and the alcoholic gibberish of the flop house, is the best example of the outrageous authority of publication.

The narrative of *Finnegans Wake* is propelled by the pressure to publicize what is hidden and secret, both literally, as in the appearance of HCE's story in the "Mercy Cordial Mendicants' Sitterdag–Zindeh–Munaday Wakeschrift" (205.16), and perversely, as in the silhouetted (on their window blind) publication of the Earwickers' copulation ("Casting such shadows to Persia's blind! The man in the street can see the coming event. Photoflashing it far too wide. It will be known through all Urania soon" [583.14]). The publication of private events is the thematic equivalent of sexual exhibitionism, which, perhaps, functions as the controlling perversion in *Finnegans Wake*, analogous to the role of sado-masochism in *Ulysses*.

The condition of idle talk and the thrust toward publication in *Finnegans Wake* manifest a self that has lost touch with its authentic being, and that takes its opinions and feelings from a disembodied, soulless public. According to Heidegger, this is the ontological condition of inauthenticity that constitutes everyday Being-in-the-world. The characters of Joyce's *Dubliners* are engaged in various degrees of resistance to this enthrallment to otherness, yet even the sensitive, intelligent Gabriel Conroy is a somnambulant dispenser of idle talk. When his inane gallantries are punctured by Lily's bitter retort, he is shaken. His dinner speech is a triumph of empty, rhetorical flourish ("Those days might, without exaggeration, be called spacious days: and if they are gone beyond recall let us hope, at least, that in gatherings such as this we shall speak of them with pride and affection, still cherish in our hearts the memory of those dead and gone great ones whose fame the world will not willingly let die" [*D*, p. 203]). When Gretta's poignant memory of the dead Michael Furey invests his hollow words with sharply personal meaning, Gabriel is painfully awakened from his burial in inauthentic existence.

The inauthenticity of the Self is a major theme in *Finnegans Wake*. "When is a man not a man?" asks Shem, as he teases his brothers and sisters with "the first riddle of the universe" (170.4). Their answers, which include references to loss of life, faith, virility, and consciousness are all incorrect, the correct answer being "when he is a . . . Sham" (170.23). The predominance of lying, plagiarizing, evading straight answers, and faking innocence suggests that inauthenticity in the work is a function of the interaction of guilt and idle talk. Guilt generates idle talk as a defense; idle talk represents an inauthentic guilty being. Jacques Lacan calls the discourse of the psychoanalytic patient a kind of inauthentic idle talk, "the empty Word, where the subject seems to be talking in vain about someone who, even if he were his spitting image, can never become one with the assumption of his desire."[12] The issue of HCE's specific guilt or innocence is finally a sham issue in a universe where everyone is guilty. The search for the "facts," the "objective" truth, is a red herring that conceals the real issue: the universal guilt resulting from the oedipal relationship to one's parents, the Original Sin descended from Adam and Eve. *"Hirp! Hirp! for their Missed Understandings!"* (175.27), writes Shem in his revised version of the "Ballat of Perce-Oreille," in which he acknowledges the inevitability of the fall (*"Cleftfoot from Hempal must tumpel, Blamefool Gardener's bound to fall; Broken Eggs will poursuive bitten Apples for where theirs is Will there's his Wall"* [175.17]). The misunderstanding of guilt in *Finnegans Wake* arises from the mistaken notion that the sin is a specific deed, a particular social or moral infraction, a legal or psycho-analytic "case," as it were. The Wakean treatment of the mysterious sin as "case" gives rise to a bilingual pun: the German word *Fall* means "fall" and "case" or "instance." In I.3 a German reporter, a certain Herr Betreffender, reports on "Der Fall Adams for the Frankofurto Siding, a Fastland payrodicule" (70.5). *Betreffen,* of course, means "about" or "concerning," as though the reporter writing of the fall of Adam and the case of Adam were really documenting his own case as though it belonged to another. Martin Heidegger writes of this failure to confront guilt truly and the tendency to regard guilt as something alien to the self but belonging to others. "The common sense of the 'they' knows only the satisfying of manipulable rules and public norms and the failure to satisfy them. It reckons up infractions of them and tries to balance them off. It has slunk away from its ownmost Being-guilty so as to be able to talk more loudly about making 'mistakes.' "[13]

Heidegger speaks of the condition of the fall, *Verfallen,* not as a traditional moral lapse, but as a falling away from one's authentic self into a state of "otherness" or inauthenticity.

The questions of the fall of man, guilt, and the self, finally constitute a closed circle in the *Wake.* Primordial guilt prompts evasion and the search for guilt in the "other," which results in the inauthen-ticity of the self. Inauthenticity, in turn, itself constitutes the fall of man in the modern intellectual arena that has dealt the most serious blow to a cherished belief in the primacy of man's self-knowledge, and his consequent free will.

The reader's difficulty in "relating" to *Finnegans Wake,* in identi-fying with its characters, stands in an inverse relationship to the ease and clarity with which we understand Joyce's boy protagonists in "The Sisters," "Araby," "An Encounter," and young Dedalus in *Portrait.* These young characters are accessible to us because they struggle earnestly to locate their authentic being through their initial encounters with death and guilt; the reader relates to them because they relate to themselves. In contrast, Joyce's mature figures like the paralyzed Dub-liners, the priests of *Portrait,* and the adult Stephen and Bloom (at times), approach the type of fraudulent "public" person exemplified by Shaun. Shaun's role as politician in III.1 and preacher in III.2 are suitable roles for this postman who carries and steals the letters of others, this pedant who spouts the words of others and claims that others are responsible for his acts ("Forgive me, Shaun repeated from his liquid lipes, not what I wants to do a strike of work but it was condemned on me premitially by Hieark Books and Chief overseer Cooks in their Eusebian Concordant Homilies and there does be a power coming over me that is put upon me from on high" [409.33]). Shaun distorts the notion of "divine mission," which in Christ exemplifies authentic being, the acceptance of responsibility and the confrontation of one's guilt and mortality. As anti-Christ, Shaun is a hyprocritical pharisee who projects his own lewdness on others and then threatens them with castigation ("Lay your lilylike long his shoulder but buck back if he buts bolder and just hep your homely hop and heed no horning but if you've got some brainy notion to raise cancan and rouse commotion I'll be apt to flail that tail for you till it's borning" [436.33]).

Wakean figures are the products of an aesthetic theory informed not by Aquinas's *integritas, consonantia,* and *claritas,* but by the powerful intellectual currents that swept early-twentieth-century Europe and laid waste Cartesian certainty. The assertion of *cogito ergo sum* was weakened by evidence of the ex-centricity of the ego: the manifestations of the unconscious and the gap that bars the individual from true self-knowledge. In *Finnegans Wake* Joyce presents this new status of man by transferring the arena of self-knowledge from the epiphany to the dream, where the self knows itself not through brilliant flashes of light and insight, but through anxiously constructed labyrinthian puzzles that yield only to the labored interpretation of Florrie's contraries.

TRUTH

The quest in *Finnegans Wake,* like the quest in *Portrait* and *Ulysses,* explores the problem of knowing and the nature of the truth that is accessible to man. Stephen Dedalus's affinity for Aquinas in *Portrait* first suggests that Joyce understood epistemology to stand at the nexus of art and philosophy. The spectacular stylistic innovations of the later *Ulysses* and *Finnegans Wake* respond not only to a holistic view of man's everyday activities and thoughts, but also to a growing awareness of the complexity, as well as the limitations, imposed on human knowledge by our intellectual history, language, and man's own unconscious.

As Wakean narrators compulsively recount certain events in *Fin-*

negans Wake, the "truth" of the event is ever lost in the interpretation. But if the true nature of the event is hopelessly elusive, the nature of the speaker is revealed in his interpretation of the event. The relationship of HCE and ALP, a topic of ceaseless curiosity and gossip throughout the work, receives extensive reporting in three chapters: the washerwomen's gossip of Anna Livia Plurabelle in I.8, the tale of Tristan and Isolde in II.4, and the account of the Earwicker's nocturnal activity in III.4. Each of the three major books in *Finnegans Wake* therefore concludes with a chapter describing the love relationship between the principal male and female figure in the work. But the three accounts stress different aspects of the relationship:

> 1. The washerwomen of I.8 report HCE's gloomy withdrawal ("hungerstriking all alone and holding doomsdag over hunselv" [199.4]) and ALP's sleepless, tireless efforts to restore him.
> 2. The version of II.4 stresses the male's athletic prowess in love-making ("when, as quick, is greased pigskin, Amoricas Champius, with one aragan throust, druve the massive of virilvigtoury flshpst the both lines of forwards (Eburnea's down, boys!) rightjingbangshot into the goal of her gullet" [395.35]).
> 3. The third account (III.4) emphasizes the brutishness and ineffectuality of the father ("Man looking round, beastly expression, fishy eyes, paralleliped homoplatts, ghazometron pondus, exhibits rage" [559.22]).

The truth-value of these accounts is subject to the interpretive functions of the narratives. While each narrator emphasizes various aspects of the HCE-ALP relationship, their accounts are merely interpretations colored by their own feelings, fears, and biases. The accounts yield more reliable information about the narrators themselves, than about the couple under discussion. The washerwomen tell the marital history and crises of the Earwickers with the aplomb of peers. They are neither intimates nor strangers, but earthy, experienced gossips, interested in the emotional strains and adjustments of the couple's relationship. As women, they are frankly sympathetic toward ALP. The four old men of II.4 are historians. Appropriately, they recount the relationship of HCE and ALP in such images of political romance as the love affairs of Tristan, Parnell, Napoleon, Egyptian royalty, and Boucicault's rebels. As impotent old men ("beautiful sister misters" [393.17], "saltwater widowers" [387.17], "four dear old heladies" [386.14]), their interest in the couple is nostalgic and frankly pornographic, as they admire Tristan's erotic assault with the brutish enthusiasm of fans at an American football game. Their memories are tinged with bitter-sweet regret at their crude collegiate exploits and lost power. In contrast, their narration as the four bedposts of III.4 has the passionless objectivity of stage directions or chess game notations ("Man with nightcap, in bed, fore. Woman, with curlpins, hind. Discovered. Side point of view. First position of harmony. Say! Eh? Ha! Check action" [559.20]). While the love-making of II.4 is related with salivating gusto, the copulation of III.4 is witnessed through the eye of the professional observer: the social worker recording the Porter's living condition, the lawyer reciting the unsavory precedents of Honophrius and other degenerates, the tour guide describing the landscape of the couple's private parts, and the gambler watching the illegal horse race ("That trainer's trundling! Quick, pay up!" [583.25]). Viewed with such businesslike acumen, the sexual experience of HCE ends with his "weeping worry-bound on his bankrump" (590.3)—an appropriate ending for a chapter devoted to "those good old lousy days gone by" (555.5).

Questions of sincerity and authenticity are topics of discussion by Joyce as early as the conclusion of *Portrait*.

> —Did the idea ever occur to you, Cranly asked, that Jesus was not what he pretended to be?
> —The first person to whom that idea occurred, Stephen answered, was Jesus himself. (*P*, p. 242)

Yet the sincerity and veracity of the narrator of *Portrait* is never an issue. In fact, the narrator has been so perfectly identified with Joyce that readers and critics alike feel at liberty to use *Portrait* as a biographical source. In *Finnegans Wake* the nature of the work as a representation of a dream confirms the impossibility of truth in discourse ("Thus the unfacts, did we possess them, are too imprecisely few to warrant our certitude, the evidencegivers by legpoll too untrustworthily irreperible" [57.16]). The "evidencegivers" are indeed untrustworthy, as untrustworthy as the psychoanalytic patient telling the history that hides the oedipal trauma ("Be these meer marchant taylor's fablings of a race referend with oddman rex? Is now all seenheard then forgotten?" [61.28]).

In evaluating the function of this preponderance of untruth as it determines the status of the work's epistemology, an examination of the debate between St. Patrick and the Archdruid Berkeley in Book IV is helpful.

Much of the difficulty of this puzzling passage is due to the density and obscurity of the language; it is not always clear who is speaking to whom. But James Atherton, thankfully, has minimized the confusion by providing an early draft of the passage.

The archdruid then explained the illusions of the colourful world, its furniture, animal, vegetable and mineral, appearing to fallen men under but one reflection of the several iridal gradations of solar light, that one which it had been unable to absorb, while for the seer beholding reality, the thing as in itself it is, all objects showed themselves in their true colours, resplendent with the sextuple glory of the light actually retained within them.[14]

Atherton goes on to observe, "This bears little resemblance to Berkeley's theory of acquired visual perception, for Berkeley held that the things which are called sensible material objects are not external but exist in the mind."[15] The archdruid-Patrick debate is one of the earliest known fragments of *Finnegans Wake*. Its importance to the epistemology of the entire work is suggested by Joyce's designation of the debate as both defense and indictment of *Finnegans Wake* in the famous letter to Frank Budgen.[16]

Serving as exemplars for the archdruid's thesis, the archdruid, clad in his rainbow-hued mantle, represents the seer, while Patrick, interestingly, embodies the fallen man whose world looks monochromatic. Besides yielding comments on aesthetics and imperialism,[17] the debate distinguishes between natural and mystical epistemologies. The archdruid's seer beholds the reality of nature by letting objects reveal themselves to him in their true colors, an approach quite similar to Heidegger's concept of "truth." " 'Truth' is not the mark of some correct proposition made by a human 'subject' in respect of an 'object' and which then—in precisely what sphere we do not know—counts as 'true'; truth is rather the revelation of what-is, a revelation through which something 'overt' comes into force."[18] For Heidegger, *the essence of truth is freedom*,[19] and freedom reveals itself in the "letting-be" of what-is, not in a negative sense of renunciation or indifference, but as participation in the revealed nature of what-is. Patrick rejects the archdruid's natural concept of revelation in favor of an anagogical interpretation of the phenomenal world, as in the understanding of the Trinity by the shamrock ("the sound sense sympol in a weedwayed-

wold" [612.29]). Patrick's concept of revelation is therefore theological. It refers to the Divine whose Mystery contains the "truth" or true
reality, while the seer's vision, like Heidegger's understanding of
"truth," belongs to human experience.

Interestingly the notion of "fallen man" in the debate is related to
ways of seeing the world, rather than to moral or ethical acts. In fact,
what Patrick fails to recognize, the "true inwardness of reality, the Ding
hvad in idself id est" (611.21), seems to be precisely the *id,* the seat of
man's morally and ethically negative impulses. The fall of man in
Finnegans Wake seems to be an ontological matter above all: the failure
to accept the complex and guilty truth about himself and his human
condition.

While debating these weighty questions, the two great spokesmen
of the spiritual life, archdruid and saint, are engaged in a struggle whose
forms range from the imperialistic conflict to the gambling match.
Imperialism and gambling share the common goal of conquest. Diverse
images merge the two activities, as when Muta and Juva bet on the
horses "burkeley buy" and "Eurasian Generalissimo" (610.12), and
someone yells "Shoot" (610.33)–the signal to start the horse race or
the assassination. The link between the Buckley–Russian General confrontation and the gambling activities of the Berkeley-Patrick debate is
also expressed in the implicit pun of *crap game,* with its simultaneous
reference to defecation and gambling ("Sweating on to stonker and
throw his seven" [612.33]). Someone, probably Patrick, is squatting on
the ground. Like the Russian General, he may be wiping his arse ("hims
hers" [612.25]) with a bit of Irish sod, a synthetic chamois handkerchief, or a handful of shamrocks ("wipenmeselps gnosegates a hand-
caughtscheaf of synthetic shammyrag to hims hers" [612.24]). Then
again, he may merely be searching for a shamrock on the ground with
which to demonstrate the Holy Trinity, or perhaps for the Irishman's
pot of gold at the end of the rainbow ("ruinboon pot" [612.20]). The
rainbow pot may also be the kitty of a bridge game ("four three two
agreement" [612.26]) in which heart is trump ("cause heart to be
might" [612.26]), and the object of Patrick's search on the ground
may be a shamrock-shaped club. The final assault appears to be both
physical and psychological: shooting or impaling the opponent's arse
("His Ards" [612.35]), thumping him over the head with a club or
poker from the card games, or trumping his cards, Ace, or hearts ("he

shuck his thumping fore features apt the hoyhop of His Ards" [612.35]). And, then again, the loser may merely have forfeited ("fore features") the game or his life.

Even the archdruid and the saint, trying to understand the nature of being and knowing, are lost in the inauthenticity of a world concerned with power rather than with truth. Man cannot simultaneously worship the sun and revel in the splendor of the rainbow, while searching for the pot of gold at its base. "Good safe firelamp!" and "Goldselforelump!" (613.1) may cancel each other out by "neutrolysis" like the colors green and red when they are mixed (612.22).

The rainbow itself is a complex and versatile image in the *Wake,* quite unrestricted by its conventional symbolic functions. An important element in the dense biblical imagery of the Noah myth, the rainbow occurs after the deluge, a sign of salvation ("the skysign of soft advertisement" [4.13]) as well as the reflection and product of the sin and destruction that preceded it. Saved Noah falls again when his sons, or Dublin's Guinness brothers, brew rainbow-colored liquor ("rhubarbarous maundarin yellagreen funkleblue windigut diodying applejack" [171.16]) by "arclight" (3.13). At another occasion of great drinking, Finnegan's wake, the Sunday King presides in a "seven-coloured's soot" (277.1) over the iridescent drink or urine ("Will ye nought would wet your weapons" [277, F3]) of the ancient rainbow warriors, Roe, Williams, Bewey, Greene, Gorham, McEndicoth and Vyler (277, F4). Rainbows are created by sunlight and liquids; and such liquids in the *Wake*—deluge, liquor, and urine—are elements of the fall. The temptresses who tease and torment fathers and sons also take form as rainbow girls at times. Rose, Sevilla, Citronelle, Esmeralde, Pervinca, Indra, and Viola (223.6), must be won in II.1 by guessing the color riddle—another correlation of colors and epistemology like that found in the Berkeley-Patrick debate. Still another image totally contradicts the meaning the rainbow assumes in the archdruid's thesis. At the end of III.4, HCE is described as "a chameleon at last, in his true falseheaven colours from ultraviolet to subred tissues" (590.7). The rainbow colors hide the true nature of things rather than reveal the thing-in-itself, as to Berkeley's seer. Furthermore, the combative spirit of the archdruid-Berkeley relationship is here embodied in the rainbow as weapon, "His reignbolt's shot," and as a "grand tryomphal arch" (590.9–10).

In a convoluted way, this prevalent association of the rainbow image with the fall modifies the archdruid's thesis. We are left with the impression that the seer, who beholds the colorful world in its seven-hued splendor, really sees the fall of man, while the fallen man is one who wears "monkblinkers" (612.21), like Patrick, and sees only one hue, refusing to acknowledge the full spectrum of primordial guilt.

The reference to Matthew Arnold's aesthetic theory[20] in the archdruid-Patrick debate suggests that the discussion of the nature and perception of reality has important aesthetic implications as well. The portrait of the artist in *Finnegans Wake* is so antipodal to that in *Portrait* that it is almost unrecognizable. Instead of a "priest of eternal imagination, transmuting the daily bread of experience into the radiant body of everliving life" (*P*, p. 221), we find low Shem, the sham, shamman, and devil, transmuting his excrement into art. Yet this transformation of the artist from soaring Icarus to subterranean rodent living in "pure mousefarm filth" (183.4) is consistent with Joyce's shifting focus over the years. In *Portrait* Stephen's body is "illclad, illfed, louseeaten" (*P*, p. 234), while his soul is held aloof from the squalor of the rabble. But this heroic pose leaves him vulnerable to the conceit and pretensions of the spiritual aristocrat: "Reproduction is the beginning of death," quotes Temple to Stephen—"Do you feel how profound that is because you are a poet?" (*P*, p. 231).

As Joyce's interest shifted from consciousness to the unconscious, he was increasingly forced to recognize the inauthenticity and self-delusion that the artist shares with the philistine. In the world of the dream, every individual is a demon and an angel, a pharisee and a holy man, a charlatan and an artist. The artist enjoys no corner on truth; he merely constructs more elaborate and elegant myths and lies more convincingly than the man on the street. Only when he recognizes and exposes his own fakery, and, like Joyce, acknowledges the artistic creation as a "song of alibi" (193.30), does he arrive at some truth of the human condition: the paradoxical truth suggested by Heidegger when he writes "Dasein is equiprimordially both in the truth and in untruth."[21] Joyce comes to maturity when he replaces the artist's epiphany as the moment of truth with the oedipal insight into his own blindness and hypocrisy.

The question of knowledge in *Finnegans Wake* takes its most mythic and primitive form in the riddles that dot the book: the Prankquean's "why do I am alook alike a poss of porterpease?" (21.18), Shem's "when is a man not a man?" (170.5), the heliotrope riddle of the game of colors in II.1, and the question, "where was a hovel not a havel" (231.1). It is interesting that neither these riddles, nor ones found in Joyce's earlier works, the Athy riddle in *Portrait* and the fox and grandmother riddle in *Ulysses,* are ever answered correctly. Riddles require no outside or new information. They generally deal with the familiar, the obvious, but they do require that new connections be made between perfectly ordinary things. In other words, riddles presuppose knowledge, but they require recognition. Oedipus easily guesses the Sphinx's riddle as "man"; he does not recognize that the references to feet and walking have a highly singular meaning for him and that the riddle depicts his own past, present, and future. Perhaps Wakean figures fail to guess riddles precisely because they lack the power of recognition, or because they are blind to their own conditions. Shem/Glugg can only guess the heliotrope riddle if he recognizes his enemy twin's dominance and sexual triumph, since Shaun/Chuff represents the sun whom the rainbow girls adore. The "home," which is the answer to the hovel riddle, is associated with guilty sexual experiences and wishes, as Benstock points out.[22] The self-awareness and self-recognition are too painful, and the questioned fail and err instead.

The knowledge that is finally sought by all Wakean figures is the truth of their own being, the answer to the question that lies at the heart of the Oedipus myth: "Who am I?" Wilden writes of the oedipal question, "To pose the question at all is the subject's way of recognizing that he is neither who he thinks he is nor what he wants to be, since at the level of the *parole vide* he will always find that he is another."[23] Like *Ulysses, Finnegans Wake* is a quest for the nature of the self—a quest conducted in error and doubt because the truth will not be comforting or reassuring. Stuart Schneiderman writes, "Man's freedom, his ability to know the truth, necessitates his ability to err, to wander, not to know that he has been, not to know the continuity between what has been and what is, and therefore to be in doubt as to whether he is."[24] All figures in the *Wake* are led, like Shem, to the altar of the "cloud Incertitude" (178.31).

DEATH

Throughout Joyce's works, the alienation of his characters is delineated and focused through their relationship to death. *Dubliners* begins with the death of Father Flynn in "The Sisters," and ends with "The Dead," the story of Gabriel Conroy's dislocation from the center of his world by the discovery of dead Michael Furey's place in Gretta's memory and affection. Early in *Portrait* young Stephen fantasizes his own death and dreams of the death of Parnell. The end of *Portrait* and the beginning of *Ulysses* are bridged by the death of Stephen's mother. *Ulysses* itself is haunted by the dead or ghosts of the dead: Stephen's mother, Paddy Dignam, Bloom's suicide father, the infant Rudy, Hamlet's father, and the mythical drowned man.

Death, of course, is a major theme in *Finnegans Wake*, as the title indicates. But the deliberate ambiguity of the title, with its dual reference to the death watch and resurrection, has led to a particular critical bias toward the subject of death in the work. Death is regarded as inseparable from resurrection, with which it forms the nexus that makes the cyclical recurrence of social history possible. Society fosters myths of death and rebirth to assure its members of life's continuity — like the myths reflected in Molly's metempsychosis and the ballad of Tim Finnegan itself. Such myths minimize the "sting" of personal death which all men must anticipate, and they thereby become part of the elaborate mechanism by which man evades the stupefying recognition of his own impending death.

In the three *Dubliners* stories that deal with death, we see the death of another provide the protagonist with an insight into the inauthenticity of his own life and of those near him. While the boy in "The Sisters" angrily derides to himself the insensitive old Mr. Cotter, he himself has surprising, though involuntary, feelings toward Fr. Flynn's death ("a sensation of freedom as if I had been freed from something by his death" [D, p. 12]). Mr. Duffy in "A Painful Case" recognizes only upon Mrs. Sinico's death how his fastidiousness had masked an utter lovelessness. This recognition makes him feel "his moral nature falling to pieces" (D, p. 117). Gabriel Conroy, after presiding with such bourgeois expansiveness at the Christmas party, receives a cruel shock of self-recognition by the evocation of Michael Furey's death ("He saw himself as a ludicrous figure, acting as a pennyboy for his aunts, a nervous, well-meaning sentimentalist, orating to vulgarians and idealising his own clownish lusts, the pitiable fatuous fellow he had caught a glimpse of in the mirror" [D, p. 220]).

The title of "A Painful Case," taken from the newspaper account, emphasizes the objective and businesslike attitude people take toward the death of others. While reminding them of their own flawed and mortal existence, the death of another evokes mingled feelings of guilt and relief in the mourners.

Bloom, in *Ulysses,* muses on the reassurance that the death of others brings to the living. Of an old woman watching the funeral procession, he thinks, "Thanking her stars she was passed over" (*U,* p. 87), and of the cemetery caretaker's demeanor, "He looks cheerful enough over it. Gives him a sense of power seeing all the others go under first" (*U,* p. 109). Bloom's own comportment toward death in "Hades" is like that toward a case of death, or death as a mishap occurring to others ("Funerals all over the world everywhere every minute. Shovelling them under by the cartload doublequick. Thousands every hour" [*U*, p. 101]).

Among the many parallels that connect I.1, the first chapter of *Finnegans Wake,* and Book IV, the last, we find a major reference to death. At the end of I.1, the mourners surround the coffin of the dead Finn MacCool, and as he tries to rise in the manner of Tim Finnegan, they soothe him back with a long address. This address reveals an absorption in the world of everyday human concerns. The mourners tell him how well he is laid out and equipped, with "all you want, pouch, gloves, flask, bricket, kerchief, ring and amberulla, the whole treasure of the pyre" (24.32). They report his posthumous fame ("Your fame is spreading like Basilico's ointment since the Fintan Lalors piped you overborder" [25.9]). They bring news of home and family ("Everything's going on the same or so it appeals to all of us, in the old holmsted here" [26.25]).

This attention to practical matters is virtually a boast to the dead of one's own energetic belonging to the world of the living. It is another reassurance of one's own survival and an evasion of the recognition that death will eventually claim the individual for itself. This evasion of death as a unique human possibility confronting the self is an expression of the individual's inauthenticity, an inauthentic Being-towards-Death, which, according to Martin Heidegger, belongs to the fall of man (*Verfallen*) into "otherness."

In Dasein's public way of interpreting, it is said that 'one dies,' because everyone else and oneself can talk himself into saying that "in no case is it I myself," for this "one" is *the "nobody."* 'Dying' is levelled off to an occurrence which reaches Dasein, to be sure, but belongs to nobody in particular. . . . Dying, which is essentially mine in such a way that no one can be my representative, is perverted into an event of public occurrence which the "they" encounters.[25]

Perhaps only in the twentieth century, in the aftermath of the nineteenth-century *death of God,* is an authentic Being-toward-Death even possible. There is various evidence that Joyce may have intended the anticipation of death to provide the controlling frame of *Finnegans Wake.* "As Joyce informed a friend later, he conceived of his book as the dream of old Finn, lying in death beside the river Liffey and watching the history of Ireland and the world—past and future—flow through his mind like flotsam on the river of life."[26] According to Stanislaus Joyce's diary, Joyce also read Leo Tolstoy's *Sebastopol Sketches* with interest. "The description of Praskukhin's random thoughts on the verge of death stirred him to try to write down the random thoughts of someone on the verge of sleep."[27] Although there is no definite evidence that Joyce read Tolstoy's "The Death of Ivan Ilych," that work is one of modern literature's most penetrating studies of authentic and inauthentic Being-towards-Death in dialectical con-flict—much like that in *Finnegans Wake* itself.

Although there is probably nothing on earth quite like an Irish wake, the mourners of Ivan Ilych behave much like the mourners at Finn's wake, with their nervous retreat into practical matters ("I consider it an affectation to say that my grief prevents my attending to practical affairs. On the contrary, if anything can—I won't say console me, but—distract me, it is seeing to everything concerning him"[28]). Anna Liva, of course, shares in the mourners' practical concerns ("Gramp-upus is fallen down but grinny sprids the boord" [7.8]). ALP is the hostess serving refreshments at the wake, the priestess serving her husband's body to the mourners, and Isis gathering the fragments of Osiris together for restoration. The mourners at Finn's wake project ALP's own death, but evasively, as the death of another, bound to come, but not here and now ("There'll be bluebells blowing in salty sepulchres the night she signs her final tear. Zee End. But that's a world of ways away" [28.27]). When that moment arrives in the middle of ALP's final monologue, however, her comportment, like that of Ivan Ilych, reveals an authentic Being-towards-Death.

Most of ALP's final monologue, presumably addressed to HCE, is about that world of practical concerns which informs the gossip of

Finnegans Wake. Near the end of her speech, however, she recognizes that her "time is come" (627.13), and from then on she speaks mainly to herself, husband and children having become "they." Her final words address her father—death itself. Her change from intense involvement in the world of cares and concern with others, to a sudden total aloofness, indicates a recognition that in the face of death, the individual entirely loses her connection to others ("When it stands before itself in this way, all its relations to any other Dasein have been undone"[29]). The noisy merrymaking and brawling at Finn's wake contrasts all the more sharply with the stark solitude of ALP at the end.

ALP's recognition of her separation from the living accounts for her otherwise inexplicable repudiation of husband and children, who, moments before, had been the object of her concern and love. Furthermore, she recognizes that her family will be unable to grasp the experience of her dying, and will evade that recognition by banding together as the busy living ("A hundred cares, a tithe of troubles and is there one who understands me? . . . They'll never see. Nor know. Nor miss me" [627.14, 35]). Death singles out the individual in such a way that concern for other people becomes meaningless ("All me life I have been lived among them but now they are becoming lothed to me" [627.16]). Her total repudiation ("How small it's all" [627.20]) echoes the thoughts of the dying Ivan Ilych ("all that had then seemed joys now melted before his sight and turned into something trivial and often nasty"[30]).

In her final moments, ALP experiences that anxiety that is not a momentary fear of death, but a recognition, anticipation, and acceptance of "the 'nothing' of the possible impossibility of its existence."[31] When ALP opens herself to the anxiety of confronting annihilation, she recognizes that death in this case is hers ("my only") not to be evaded, but to be embraced as her ultimate, personal, unique, human possibility ("And it's old and old it's sad and old it's sad and weary I go back to you, my cold father, my cold mad father, my cold mad feary father, till the near sight of the mere size of him, the moyles and moyles of it, moananoaning, makes me seasilt saltsick and I rush, my only, into your arms" [627.36]). Clive Hart's carefully drawn parallels between ALP's monologue and "Eveline" show the extent to which ALP's last moments reverse the paralysis theme that informs Joyce's early works. If Eveline is doomed to continued death-in-life, then ALP finds life-in-death; the children learn in the homework lesson that "a poor soul is between shift and shift ere the death he has lived through becomes the life he is to die into" (293.2). *The Wasteland* references at the beginning of the chapter ("Sandhyas! Sandhyas! Sandhyas!" [593.1]), confirm the concern with spiritual death and rebirth in this chapter, although ALP's mystical surrender to the ultimate Other is neither Eastern nor Christian, but pagan and primitive. The heavy critical emphasis on the circularity of *Finnegans Wake,* and on ALP's vital reemergence in the first line of the work, tends to obscure the apocalyptic anguish of her death.

If Joyce's figures seem to lose the palpable humanity they enjoy in his earlier works, it is only because the later work shows a complex life in which the everyday Being-in-the-world is only one of many ontological conditions explored. *Finnegans Wake* is a work that affirms life's continuous cycles over cosmic distance, and in which Vico's birth, marriage, and death role by in impeccable and perpetual succession. But the inexorable progress from cradle to grave, from innocence to experience, is terrifying for the individual caught up in the cyclical machinery. The *Wake* is also about that fear, about the resistance of Wakean figures to change and decline, about their reluctance to recognize their guilt and mortality, and about their escape into the defenses, disguises, illusions, and myths available to them in the dream. Dreams go by contraries, Florrie says. Molly Bloom utters her majestic yes yes yes to life as Eros. ALP whispers hers fearfully, ecstatically to Death.

DREAM
AND
POETRY

THE DREAM PROCESS

The critical assessment of the language of *Finnegans Wake,* with its lexical deviance and semantic density, depends finally on an understanding of the status and function of words in the dream. Those serious *Wake* critics who have judged the linguistic complexity of the work as superfluous—ornamental, perhaps, but nonfunctional—have also harbored serious misconceptions about the nature of the dream and the expression of the dream in *Finnegans Wake.* In his 1931 essay in *Axel's Castle,* Edmund Wilson complained that *Wake* language at times gives the book a "mere synthetic complication." He went on to write, "And as soon as we are aware of Joyce himself systematically embroidering on his text, deliberately inventing puzzles, the illusion of the dream is lost."[1] Thirty years later, Clive Hart echoed Wilson's criticism in his conviction that *Finnegans Wake* is an essentially simple narrative, burdened with a "massive superstructure of interwoven motifs."[2]

Both Wilson and Hart misrepresent two crucial aspects of the nature of the dream. The first is the status of knowledge, particularly self-knowledge, in the dream. When Wilson remarks that *Finnegans Wake* plunges us directly into "the consciousness of the dreamer itself,"[3] he voices the same contradiction found in Hart's statement,

"The Dreamer is omniscient."[4] The dream is precisely the arena in which the conscious subject discovers himself enthralled to another, who is himself, and yet remains inaccessible, barred from his conscious thought. The dreamer is not unitary, or conscious, or omniscient. Therefore, if *Finnegans Wake* can be assumed to represent a dream, traditional notions of point of view do not apply. The vantage point of the work is not an area of consciousness, but rather is a place where the unconscious—the essentially "unknowable" self—tries to communicate with the dreamer's conscious self. The unconscious is unknowable except by the processes or operations it employs to reach the surface of the dreamer's mind. If we assume that the dreamer can be found there, where conflicts and tensions appear in the language of *Finnegans Wake*, we have made a giant step toward locating his function, as well as having rendered nugatory the question of his identity.

Both Wilson's and Hart's concepts of the dream form in *Finnegans Wake* are essentially incompatible with the complicated, deviant language of the work. Hart determines three levels of dreaming in *Finnegans Wake*. He contends that Joyce patterned these levels on the AUM states of the Upanishads and that the descending dream levels represent a "mystical pilgrimage of Earwicker's spirit, seeking salvation through self-knowledge."[5] The Freudian dream, however, is not a progressive penetration into the unconscious[6]—a peeling back of layers or lifting of veils to disclose successive states of psychic truth. In the dream, the unconscious manifests itself through certain structural operations, such as the ordering and organization of materials, preferential selections, and substitutions—the processes Freud called distortion, displacement, and condensation. In other words, the dream is a rebus—a puzzle with an important linguistic component. Freud's dream-analyses revolve time and again around key words (*"propyl, propyls . . . propionic acid . . . trimethylamin"* in the dream of Irma's injection, such puns as *"norekdal"* and *"gen Italien,"* and the marvelous multivalent pun of *"Espe"* in the Wolf Man's dream[7]). When Wilson laments that the language of the *Wake* spoils the "illusion of the dream," he calls for an imitative form of the dream, presuming that the dream has a model form. Yet insofar as the dream is a rebus, Joyce's "deliberately inventing puzzles" imitates precisely the activity of dream-work.[8]

Finnegans Wake is not merely the "illusion" of a dream, or the "surface" of a dream, as it were. The work, in fact, explores the relationship between the conscious and the unconscious, and the strange, cunning, antagonistic communication that is effected between them in dreams. A special language had to be forged for this purpose, as Joyce explained to Harriet Shaw Weaver, "One great part of every human existence is passed in a state which cannot be rendered sensible by the use of wideawake language, cutanddry grammar, and goahead plot."[9]

In its simplest description, the language of *Finnegans Wake* is a combination of prose and poetry. But the linear narrative line and the poetic forms embedded in it work at cross-purposes to one another. It is the function of the labyrinthian prose to lead the hearer astray, to reduce the issue at hand to confusion, to digress until the main point of the narrative is lost. At the same time the poetic forms, the metonymies, puns, klang-associations, neologisms, and portmanteau words short-circuit that intention and erupt in spontaneous, involuntary confessions in the midst of the narration. The first question of the "nightly quisquiquock" (126.6) or "Who's Who?" in I.5 unfolds over some fourteen nonstop pages of eulogizing description of the subject, Finn MacCool, the "secondtonone myther rector and maximost bridgesmaker" (126.10). Yet the individual items of the long catalogue of attributes expose some of the "false hood of a spindler web" (131.18) through klang-associations and other devices. This exposure is familiar and often literal, as, for example, when we hear that the hero "shows he's fly to both demisfairs but thries to cover up his tracers" (129.21). Showing that he's a fly, insect, or earwig simply identifies Finn Mac-Cool with HCE, while showing his fly to the two disreputable women is the exhibitionism at which the three soldiers surprise him.

In devising a language to explore the world of the dream, Joyce made a discovery that was facilitated by the works of Freud, and whose full implications have only recently been explored by psychoanalysts like Jacques Lacan and linguists like Roman Jakobson. This discovery was the correspondence between traditional poetic devices and the processes of dream-formation. When the unconscious communicates with the conscious in a dream, it uses such operations as displacement, condensation, and distortion, allowing the shifting of meaning and the expression of several meanings at once. The poet also uses verbal structures that allow words to mean many things at once—stylistic tropes such as metaphor, metonymy, and synecdoche.[10]

These psychological and poetic forms are not only functional, but are aesthetically pleasing as well, which explains why so many of the dreams in Freud's dream book sound like small poems or fictions. In *Finnegans Wake* Joyce clearly endeavors to allow the language its fullest scope both functionally and aesthetically. Like a poem, or a dream, we should ask of the work not only what it means, but also how it means.

DISPLACEMENT

Novices to *Finnegans Wake* might well note that the language is riddled with "errors"—misspellings, nonsense words, malaproprisms. They would be right, of course, but only if they took them as seriously as Freud took "errors" in his famous treatise on errors, "The Psychopathology of Everyday Life."[11] Joyce uses such deviations and word play for a legitimate psychological purpose—to correct the conscious untruths of speakers with unconscious truths. This technique is by no means new in *Finnegans Wake*; Bloom occasionally reveals a repressed fear or guilt by a slip of the tongue, as when he inadvertently substitutes "admirers" for "advisors" in a reference that reminds him of Boylan's relationship to Molly (*U*, p. 313). In *Ulysses* these slips occur infrequently and deliberately. In *Finnegans Wake* they occur so densely that they become the norm rather than the occasional blunder.

One of Joyce's most frequently used "errors" in *Finnegans Wake* is the klang-association, in which the sound of a word or phrase instantly recalls another, similar in sound but not necessarily in meaning. The density of klang-associations in the *Wake* frequently generates a line of "double talk," in which the line of discourse in the *Wake* recalls an association, a silent second line of discourse in the reader's mind. The two conversations are generally at odds. Attempts to paraphrase the work fail for this reason: they destroy the contrapuntal tension that exists between the written word and the resonating line of thought.

"Double talk" in *Finnegans Wake* can be readily demonstrated by a few examples. A line in HCE's conversation with the twelve customers/jurors is written, "The rebald danger with they who would bare whiteness against me I dismissem from the mind of good" (364.1). Through this sentence HCE expresses two very different thoughts at once. "The real danger with they who would bear witness against me, I dismiss them from the mind of God," suggests that HCE dismisses the threat of his slanderers and damns them. On the other hand, the "ribald danger" of the temptresses, whom HCE is rumored to have watched while they urinated, is displayed when they "bare whiteness" against him, and therefore divert him, or he diverts them, "from the mind of good" or the intention of good. In the latter case, "dismissem" might possibly refer to undoing misses or virgins ("dis"—an undoing or depriving of character, quality, or rank as in "disable" or "dishonor"), or "missem" might refer to "misseem" (an archaism denoting unbecoming action); HCE's self-righteousness is always self-defeating. He claims he should have his temptress arrested ("was she but thinking of such a thing"—presumably his alleged misconduct toward her). But the words, "was she but tinkling of such a tink" (532.28), betray that HCE's thoughts have returned to the urinating girls in Phoenix Park. The children, like their father, are prone to the same self-revealing speech. During the homework lesson they suggest, "Have your little sintalks" (269.2), a more interesting subject than syntax, to be sure. One of the brothers asks the other, "As my instructor unstrict me" (295.21)—a request apparently granted, for the homework lesson does as much to undo the strictures against sexual knowledge as to instruct. Issy's pronouncements, which are often considered inane and ridiculous, are sometimes given a fine cutting edge by the revelation of her secret thoughts. "How he stalks to simself louther and lover, immutating aperybally" (460.11) seems like an innocuous enough remark, presumably referring to her aged lover, or to HCE ("How he talks to himself, louder and lower, imitating everybody"). But the sentence simultaneously conjures up the image of an apelike or simian (simself) creature, stalking about, a loutish as well as Lutheran (louther) lover, too established in his brutishness ("immutating" or unchanging) to ascend the evolutionary ladder. Issy's wantonness is often disguised by virginal piety ("So now, to thalk thildish, thome, theated with Mag at the oilthan we are doing to thay one little player before doing to deed" [461.28]). "So now, to talk childlish, come, seated with Mag at the organ we are going to say one little prayer before going to bed," is fraught with the naughty suggestions of doing some deed with "a little player" (perhaps while seated at the oilcan?). A good many of the thoughts in *Finnegans Wake* lead to Phoenix Park and its mysterious sexual guilts. Even talk about the weather—the epitome of bland conversational subjects—conceals more serious matters in the *Wake*. What seems to be the simple comment, "Strangely cold for this season of the year," is expressed as "Strangely cult for this ceasing of the yore" (279.2), suggesting bizarre funeral rites or rites of passage.

Likewise a weather forecast doubles as a prediction for nuptial outlook; the phrase, "and incurred a sudden stretch of low pressure, mist in some parts but with local drizzles, the outlook for tomorrow . . . seemed brighter, visibility good" contains an extra dimension as expressed in the *Wake* ("and incursioned [penetrated] a sotten [drunken] retch [wretch] of low pleasure, missed in some parts but with lucal drizzles, the outlook for tomarry . . . beamed brider, his ability good" [324.31]).*

These examples of "double talk" demonstrate the process of displacement in dream-formation. In order to by-pass the dream censor, elements of high psychic intensity are displaced onto elements of little value in the dream. In *Finnegans Wake,* however, this process is reversed as banal words are replaced by piquant words: syntax/sintalks, real/rebald, thinking/tinkling, pressure/pleasure, everybody/aperybally, and cold/cult. In ordinary dreaming, the displaced matter—the highly charged, guilty, sexual thoughts—would need to be inferred through free association and analysis. Since analysis is impossible within the dream framework of *Finnegans Wake,* Joyce must have decided to make the dream transparent, as it were, by giving the reader access to the repressed material. In *Ulysses* we see the personae repressing their fearful, guilty thoughts all day, only to let them surface dramatically at night in "Circe." In *Finnegans Wake* we see the repression and revelation occur simultaneously in the same line of discourse.

These paired words that sound alike often represent extreme differences in meaning, and, at times, antonyms. The tension of the pairing is heightened because one term might be brashly profane, while its echo is sanctimonious and pure. Joyce thereby demonstrates the essential nature of repression: that blasphemous and obscene words have no particular significance without their opposites.

The expression, "boob's indulligence" (531.2), becomes irreverent only with the rhythmic and phonetic resonance of "Pope's indulgence" (boob's dull intelligence, and Pope's self-indulgence, as well as the Catholic remission of punishment due to sins). Likewise, "I popetithes thee" (326.6) refers to the financial obligation to support the Church; the echo of the sacramental words, "I baptize thee," suggests that the sacrament of baptism involves the extortion of tithes. The transcribed children's songs, "Lonedom's breach lay foulend up" (239.34) and

*Bracketed inserts mine.

"Psing a psalm of psexpeans" (242.30), suggest the unsuspected obscenity of small children only in the context of the innocent rhyme. This aspect of *Wake* language proves Bruno's dictum—"every power in nature must evolve an opposite in order to realize itself"—both in the linguistic and in the psychological realm. The principle of phonemic binary opposition and the semantic notion that signifiers have meaning only in relation to other signifiers are major cornerstones of modern linguistics. Joyce, like Freud, seems also to have believed that we would be as polymorphously perverse as babies if only we didn't feel so guilty about it and try so hard to repress it.

Judging from the most obvious of such cases—the pun on *wake* itself—it seems quite likely that puns, klang-associations, and ablaut series determine some of the larger themes and motifs in the work. Joyce's *Masterbuilder* may be a *masturbator* because the two words suggest one another. *Earwicker* is an *earwig;* Anna *Livia*, the *Liffey;* and *Isabel, is a belle*—thanks to similarities in sound. Perhaps because Earwicker is an earwig or *bug,* he is also a *bugger* or *buggered,* since buggers, like earwigs, penetrate unorthodox orifices. Because the unconscious treats words like objects, it is alive to their sounds, their literal and archaic meanings, and their uses in every known context. Words alone, therefore, can generate images and scenarios in dreams. Freud's patient, feeling himself rejected by women because of his *settled* habits, dreamt of being *settled* in a chair while trying to charm a young woman.[12] Joyce seems to have borrowed this technique from dream-work, letting words suggest entire scenes. The auditory contiguity of *letter* and *litter* may have prompted the merger of ALP as scavenger with ALP as author of the Letter, in the image of the hen scratching the Letter/litter from the dump. Verbal contiguity may likewise have brought about the *shooting* of the *shitting* Russian General. More likely the *thunder* has a *hundred* letters because of the klang-association than because of a mystical number value, and Joyce may have chosen wars and drunkenness as two manifestations of the fall because of the similarity of *battle* and *bottle*.

The tension of repression inherent in *Wake* language places a particular burden on the interpreter of the Wakean dream. In Freudian dream-analysis, the individual dream elements must be researched and traced to their source; then the function of the element in the total dream-work must be determined. Likewise, the discovery of an allusion in the *Wake* is only part of the analysis. Shaun is asked during his "psychosinology,"

—I put it to you that this was solely in his sunflower state and that his haliodraping het was why maids all sighed for him, ventured and vied for him. Hm?
—After Putawayo, Kansas, Liburnum and New Aimstirdames, it wouldn't surprise me in the very least (509.21).

It is not enough to know that "sunflower" is an allusion to Oscar Wilde, who wore a boutonniere at his trial for homosexuality.[13] Shaun's psychic state is only fully revealed if we note that he ignores the homosexual reference and replies as though "sunflower state" signified something merely geographical, like the nickname of Kansas, to him. The allusion takes on the significance of a guilty desire only through the force of the repression.

In the dream and in poetry the sounds of words are as important as their sense. The source of this common ground is the tendency of the unconscious to treat words like objects or things, to play with words in the way infants play with lettered blocks: delighting purely in their physical characteristics rather than in any message that might be formed with them. The displacements in Joyce's "double talk," "whiteness" for "witness," for example, are based not only on the disparity of their meanings, but also on the similarity of their sounds. Since words related by klang-association have contiguous sounds, they constitute a poetic metonymy.[14] The phonetic word-play in *Finnegans Wake* is therefore psychoanalytically justified, as Joyce was well aware. In another example from Shaun's interrogation, Shaun is asked, in regard to the Phoenix Park incident, "Did any orangepeelers or greengoaters appear periodically up your sylvan family tree?" (522.16). Shaun, misinterpreting "sylvan" and thereby diverting the reply from the matter at hand, replies, "It all depends on how much family silver you want for a nass-and-pair" (522.18).[15] The inquisitor indignantly asks, "Can you not distinguish the sense, prain, from the sound, bray? . . . Get yourself psychoanolised!" (522.29). He has apparently recognized the substitution of "silver" for "sylvan" as the type of phonetic metonymy that signals an unconscious displacement.

While the displacements effected by "double talk" are generally quite transparent, the need to evade the censor results in even more ingenious displacements in the work. The sin in Phoenix Park, which is the source of so much anxiety for speakers, is represented in the discourse through a displacement based on a series of synecdoches. In order to avoid all reference to the specific misdeeds committed, the incident is most often replaced by a reference to the principals, two girls and three men. William York Tindall, who, fortunately, counts things in the *Wake,* reports over two hundred such references,[16] many of them even further disguised, such as "duo of druidesses . . . and the tryonforit of Oxthievious, Lapidous and Malthouse Anthemy" (271.4). However, frequently this synecdoche is even further abbreviated, so that only the numbers "two" and "three" remain to signify the entire incident. For example, in the following instances the girls and boys appear as animals ("twalegged poneys and threehandled dorkeys" [285.13]), articles of clothing ("three surtouts wripped up in itchother's, two twin pritticoaxes" [546.15]), abstractions ("two cardinal ventures and three capitol sinks" [131.1]), and vehicles ("bikeygels and troykakyls" [567.33]). There are even instances of just the numbers themselves, as in "you too and me three" (161.30), where even the number "two" is replaced by a phonetic metonymy. This last example is surely the apex of literary indirection: the little word "too," a word virtually devoid of semantic content, used to represent a pair of tempting young women. These particular examples of synecdochic displacement demonstrate further that the unconscious interconnections between words need not be semantically determined. In the case of the "two and three" synecdoche for Phoenix Park, the numbers correspond to the count of the principals; however, they may also have been chosen because of a graphic value. Since many of the terms associated with the "two and three" refer to legs or pants ("twalegged," "sycopanties," "Legglegels in bloom," and the like) they perhaps refer to two-legged and three-legged in a Wakean version of the riddle of the Sphinx. The third leg is presumably Shaun's "supernumerary leg" (499.20). "Two and three" may therefore stand for women and men with a specific reference to their sexual difference.

The occurrence of the "two and three" synecdoche in the discourse of the *Wake* serves as a code in the sense that codes are used to protect secrets from the enemy, or from a disapproving snooper. The conscious speaker would not approve the unconscious, guilty, Phoenix Park remembrances or fantasies, and he is therefore entrusted with two neutral numbers whose significance he does not fully understand. This

particular synecdoche, therefore, represents a private code that makes
sense only in the context of the information supplied in the *Wake,* like
the rats that signified his father's financial complications to Freud's
neurotic patient.[17]   Like any code, once cracked it results in an
enormous betrayal of psychic secrets—a phenomenon the more wonder-
ful since it proves the extent to which our hidden lives are invested in
the word or even the alphabetical letter. Jacques Lacan writes, "The
claims of the spirit would remain unassailable if the letter had not in
fact shown us that it can produce all the effects of truth in man
without involving the spirit at all."[18]   In this sense, Joyce—perhaps
better than any writer of the century—knew the value of the word.

    Not all allusions with guilty associations are contained within a
private code in *Finnegans Wake,* as the frequent mention of "sunflower" and "hesitancy," catchwords for homosexuality and lying in
reference to Wilde and Pigott, demonstrate. As many of Freud's case
histories and dream-analyses show, the psyche is quick to attach words
and items of language, already invested with special meaning by the
public, to its own concerns and obsessions. All allusions to materials
external to the work—literary, biblical, historical, and autobiographical—reflect the preoccupations of Wakean figures: fraternal and paternal rivalries, incestuous wishes, the Letter, and the like. For example,
allusions to the Dublin coat of arms generally intersect with the
Phoenix Park obsession via the "two and three" reference: the coat of
arms is embellished with the figures of three flaming castles and two
women, their skirts slightly raised.

    The most notable example of synecdoche in *Finnegans Wake* is
found in the initials of HCE embedded in the three-word sequences.
The full name of HCE, Humphrey Chimpden Earwicker (we surmise), is
never stated as such in the work. Yet HCE is ubiquitous, occurring in
word sets that are seemingly arbitrary and highly diversified ("Howfor-
him chirrupeth evereachbird" [98.36], "Haroun Childeric Eggeberth"
[4.32], "Hostages and Co, Engineers" [518.16], and so on). Joyce's
use of these synecdoches may have several functions. They may indicate a repression of the thought of HCE by substituting another, less
disturbing thought in its place, with only the initials to show that HCE
ever occupied the thought at all. Conversely, certain word groups may
unconsciously recall HCE. For example, when Shaun is accused of
"homosexual catheis of empathy" (522.30), the embedded initials

suggest that perhaps Shaun is indeed guilty of homosexual incest with his father. Such use of initials in the dream has a perfectly respectable precedent in the "Espe" (S.P.) of Freud's Wolf Man.

CONDENSATION

The difference between displacement and condensation is very slight. In the first case, one element is expressed that implies or suggests another; condensation, however, preserves the simultaneous presence of two elements through superimposition. The best-known forms of condensation in *Finnegans Wake* are the portmanteau words, which are generally a composite of two phonetically similar but semantically dissimilar words, thereby expressing an unlikelihood or contradiction. For example, "collupsus" incorporates "collapse" with that which collapses, the "colossus," the seemingly invulnerable giant. In "phoenish," "finish" is co-present with "phoenix," the symbol of resurrection and rebirth. If Joyce learned this device from Lewis Carroll, he learned it well—a thousand such forms could easily be cited in the *Wake.*

Puns in *Finnegans Wake* are only incidentally entertaining, as Joyce, like Shem, seems to be "letting punplays pass to ernest" (233.19). The pun on "fly," meaning a lure in fishing and a man's trouser buttons or zipper, has multiple functions in the work. The fly pun links two important animal images of HCE, the insect (earwig) and the fish ("too funny for a fish and has too much outside for an insect" [127.2]). But the notion of a fly as lure or bait juxtaposes the fishing image with the exhibitionism of HCE by which he tempts and lures the two girls and three soldiers ("shows he's fly to both demisfairs" [129.21]). The pun therefore connects two important episodes in *Finnegans Wake:* the naming of HCE in the second chapter and the display of HCE's erection to the children in the second chapter from the end. The king asks the turnpiker "whether paternoster and silver doctors were not now more fancied bait for lobstertrapping" (31.7). The lobsters to be trapped may be the three soldiers, the "three longly lurking lobstarts" (337.20), or perhaps HCE, "the grand old greeneyed lobster" (249.3), who is also the earwig, or bait, himself. But the real lure is clearly the erect penis, topped with a condom—a flowerpot in I.2 and a "buntingcap of so a pinky on the point" (567.7) in III.4—and borne "aloft amid the fixed pikes of the hunting party" (31.1) like a colorful banner or fishing lure which "shall cast welcome" (567.11) to the hunters.

Puns are plurisigns that serve the same function in dreams as a switch on a railroad track: they move thoughts from one channel to another without hiatus. As the most economical form of "double talk," they also express simultaneous thoughts, "two thinks at a time" (583.7).

Because it employs words and images that refer to several things at once, the process of condensation in dreams corresponds to the creation of poetic metaphors. In novels and prose fiction, the use of extended metaphors is quite exceptional. Dickens, for example, introduces Twemlow in *Our Mutual Friend* as an "innocent piece of dinner-furniture that went upon easy casters and was kept over a livery stableyard." We believe in the metaphor for only a moment, however, before it becomes quite clear that Twemlow is really a harmless old gentleman who serves as a convenient and frequent dinner guest. Anna Livia Plurabelle, on the other hand, is not just *like* a river; she is the Liffey as much as she is the woman.

The ALP chapter, I.8, is virtually controlled by metaphors that create multiple frames for the section: two washerwomen gossiping about a Dublin neighbor, the Celtic banshees washing the bloody shirts of the soon-to-die heroes, the opposite banks conversing about the river, and the rival sons airing the family's dirty linen as they probe once more into the mystery of their parentage. But here, more than in any other section of the work, the metaphors will not allow for a reduction into levels of meaning; the "reality" of Anna Livia Plurabelle is suspended forever at a conjunction of images, from which she cannot be extricated. As her young girlhood, her sexual blossoming, is described, the anthropomorphic tendency of the description is poised so precisely by the river imagery that it is never allowed to dominate or to establish itself as the paramount point of reference. The infant Anna, toddling and falling into a puddle and lying there laughing with her limbs aloft is the nascent river bubbling merrily under the hawthorne trees. The bawdy image of little Anna, licked by a hound "while poing her pee" (204.12) is also the innocent picture of a dog lapping the running waters of the rivulet. Prepubescent Anna has a brush with two boy scouts, who wade through her in their bare feet before she is strong enough to support a canoe, let alone a barge. And the beautiful, erotic image of the hermit Michael Arklow, plunging his hands into Anna's streaming hair, "parting them and soothing her and mingling it" (203.24) and kissing her freckled forehead, is balanced by the image of the austere young monk, tempted in spite of himself to wash his hands and wet his lips in the sweet, cool water of the dappled brook.

Wakean metaphors cannot, and must not, be split into a point of reference and its description, or "real" and "figurative" components, without destroying the plurisignification that distinguishes dream thoughts and fantasies from waking thoughts. Unlike Stephen, the Protestant children of *Portrait* do not understand metaphors (*"Tower of Ivory,* they used to say, *House of Gold!* How could a woman be a tower of ivory or a house of gold? [*P*, p. 35]). But Finn MacCool, according to the quiz in I.6, is a house ("shows Early English tracemarks and a marigold window with manigilt lights" [127.33]), a clock ("is a horologe unstoppable and the Benn of all bells" [127.36]), writing ("shipshaped phrase of buglooking words with a form like the easing moments of a graminivorous" [128.6]), a mountain, a white-haired old man, or thorn-crowned Christ ("shows one white drift of snow among the gorsegrowth of his crown" [128.20]), a mealtime ("is Breakfates, Lunger, Diener and Souper" [131.4]), a eucharistic food ("figure right, he is hoisted by the scurve of his shaggy neck; figure left, he is rationed in isobaric patties among the crew" [133.3]), a utopia ("either eldorado or ultimate thole" [134.1]), and so on. All these things are metaphors, figurative descriptions, for Finn MacCool. At the same time, such metaphors are all we know of him and have of him. In substance, Finn MacCool, like all figures in the *Wake,* is himself a metaphor—standing for those monuments of civilization that rise and fall in *Finnegans Wake.*

In a sense, all figures in dreams are metaphors and reflections or descriptions of someone or something else. Freud writes of the Irma dream, "None of these figures whom I lighted upon by following up 'Irma' appeared in the dream in bodily shape. They were concealed behind the dream figure of 'Irma,' which was thus turned into a collective image with, it must be admitted, a number of contradictory characteristics."[19] "Bygmester Finnegan" is such a collective image. Occurring early in the work, he embodies Finn MacCool, Ibsen's Masterbuilder, Tim Finnegan, and HCE, like Solness, the father of twin sons. The line, "he seesaw by neatlight of the liquor wheretwin 'twas born" (4.33), illustrates this multiple metaphor. The first image is that of a builder looking at a level, a device used to establish a horizontal line. A level consists of a glass tube filled with alcohol or ether, which encloses a movable bubble; presumably the builder looks at this glass tube as into a crystal ball, envisioning the edifices he will erect in the future and their crashing down. The second image is a paternal fantasy, the father imagining the womb filled with amniotic fluid, bearing his progeny, his twin sons, the future fruit of his sexual erection, who will fell him at their maturity. Thirdly, the image of Tim Finnegan is suggested, the drunken hod-carrier of the ballad who looks into his glass of whiskey and sees prefigured in it his climb to the top of the building and his fall. Joyce extracts the maximum semantic possibility from his words in this line; "seesaw" relates to the image of the builder's level, to seeing in two separate time planes at once, to the unsteady reeling of the drunk, to the precariousness of fate with its untimely ups and downs, and to the warring twins, who seldom achieve equilibrium in the work. Likewise, the "neatlight of the liquor" suggests the alcohol in the tube of the level, the "neat" or unadulteratèd fluid of the womb, and Tim's straight whiskey. If Joyce, like Carroll's Humpty Dumpty, had paid his words for working extra, he soon would have been bankrupt.

SUBSTITUTABILITY

Dream logic differs from conventional logic because relationships and feelings are more important than substances and facts. For example, when small children say, "Sticks and stones may break my bones, but names will never hurt me," they not only differentiate between the physical and mental natures of sticks and names, respectively, but between their logical effects as well. If one is concerned only about one's physical safety, the saying makes good sense. Yet, the saying is precisely the child's way of defending the hurt feelings caused by the names. In the world of the dream all effects are psychological, and sticks and names can be substituted freely for one another in an attack. The assailant of the incarcerated HCE, therefore, does both for good measure. He pegs smooth stones at HCE (72.27) and calls him a list of names, on the telephone ("hello gripes" [72.20]), or crudely "hog-callering" (70.20) through the keyhole, through which he blew Quaker Oats before he started pegging stones. The specific nature of the projectiles is not important: the dreamer, like Polyphemous ("nobody-atall with Wholyphamous and build rocks over him" [73.9]), knows that rocks are not enough for "touchin his woundid feelins" (72.22), and that one needs names to call as well.

While conventional waking logic demands that events move from causes to effects, the actions of dream events can be reversible, as the incarceration theme in *Finnegans Wake* illustrates. This theme has precedents in the early works, notably in the outhouse episodes of *Portrait* and *Ulysses,* in which the "square" or the jakes is the scene not only of excretion, but also of reading, writing, mysterious sins and their attendant guilt, and paranoia.

Wakean figures are confined in a space that has many forms. For Persse O'Reilly it is "the penal jail of Mountjoy" (45.17), for Shem, "the Haunted Inkbottle" (182.31). It is a mere hole in the wall (69.5) and the garden of Eden; the magic circle of Stonehenge (69.15) or a place shared with animals, such as the cave of Polyphemous with its sheep and goats, or Noah's (178.12) ark with its "antediluvial zoo" (47.4), or Daniel's lions den ("diablen lionndub" [72.34]). It is a room on the night of the Passover ("every doorpost in muchtried Lucalizod was smeared with generous erstborn gore" [178.9]) and the cénacle in which Christ performed the Last Supper ("give him his ... thicker-thanwater to drink and his bleday steppebrodhar's into the bucket" [70.25]). It is a phone booth (72.20), a coffin, and, of course, a toilet ("a bedstead in loo thereof to keep out donkeys" [69.22] or asses— with Shem's "cheeks and trousers changing colour every time a gat croaked" [177.6]).

Both HCE and Shem are victims of incarceration. Their enclosure serves as both prison and asylum, as protection of the "nigger bloke" (177.4) against the lynch mob, and as "archicitadel" (73.24), sheltering its inmates "behind faminebuilt walls" (71.2). The attack from the outside both stimulates and inhibits creative activity on the inside. This activity is essentially transubstantiation, activity at once sacred as in communion, profane as in digestion and excretion, domestic as in cooking, mysterious as in alchemy, and artistic as in writing. For example, the state of siege ("last stage in the siegings" [73.24]), entails, among many deprivations, the extreme fear of starvation, which con-jures up the extreme remedy of cannibalism. Joyce, like Voltaire and Chaplin, recognized the comic potential of this situation, which in the *Wake* evokes reference to the assailant offering to break HCE's head and give him his own blood to drink, in communion parody, or perhaps like the cannibalistic Polyphemous, demanding "more wood alcohol to pitch in with" (70.27) and opening the "wrathfloods of his atillarery" (70.31) "without even a luncheonette interval" (70.33). Forced to be a "self valeter by choice of need" (184.11), Shem cooks up egg dishes ("whites and yolks and yilks" [184.18]) with a variety of human discharges ("Asther's mess and Huster's micture and Yellownan's embrocation and Pinkingtone's patty and stardust and sinner's tears" [184.22]). HCE, buried, or hibernating, in his watery grave, consumes his own body ("secretly and by suckage feeding on his own misplaced fat" [79.12]), as Shem, deprived of writing implements, produces ink and paper out of "his wit's waste" (185.7).

Joyce's own biography demonstrates how a Philistine public's efforts to inhibit an artist's activity may, inadvertently, foster it. Through the incarceration theme in *Finnegans Wake,* Joyce shows the relationship of society and the artist to be one of mutual aggression. If HCE's assailant hurls words and stones into the enclosure, Shem spits out (178.29) and writes graffiti or "nameless shamelessness about everybody ever he met" (182.14). The hostility of the assailant and the prisoner is represented most economically in the mirror image of the opposite sides of the keyhole: Shem voyeuristically looks out at the rainbow girls through a telescope (178.27), while the revolver looks in (179.3). The image also refers to the Buckley–Russian General episode, since the gun is aimed at a defecating ass ("had been told off to shade and shoot shy Shem should the shit show his shiny shnout" [179.5]). The action may be an aggressive response to the offensive wiping gesture of the Russian General figure, which here takes the form of Shem's verbal threat that "he would wipe alley english spooker, multaphoniaksically spuking, off the face of the erse" (178.6).

Incarceration in *Finnegans Wake* is not a novelistic event but a poetic image. Its meaning is not to be found by asking journalistic questions such as who is imprisoned by whom, where, when, and why. Any number of names, places, times, and reasons could be substituted for the answer without shedding any more light on the meaning or on the importance of the event. Freud insisted at the outset that the dream must be studied not as a whole, but in its parts, *"en détail* and not *en masse."*[20] By examining the details of the incarceration theme and by following their trail of allusions and associations, the rich and multiple meaning of the whole emerges as though from a poetic image. Structurally, the incarceration theme involves the problem of containers and orifices, the passage of substances from inside to outside or outside to inside, and the changes such passages produce. Psychologically, it concerns the simultaneous feelings of fear and anger aroused in the dreamer by these movements and changes of substance.

WIT

Regretably, the critical essay on the humor in *Finnegans Wake,* which Joyce planned to include in the sequel to *Our Exagmination,*[21] was never written. The question of Joyce's humor is complex on many counts. From the bleak and somber beginnings of *Dubliners,* Joyce's fictions became funnier with time, until the rollicking, bawdy, sophisticated wit of *Finnegans Wake* erupted in a sustained torrent during seventeen years of illness, advancing blindness, professional disappointment and frustration, and alarm over his daughter Lucia's worsening condition. Only perilous links between the literary humor and Joyce's disposition during this period can be made. The more significant connection between the comic later works and Joyce's deepening interest in the unconscious mind suggests that the humor of *Finnegans Wake* emerges as a stylistic necessity in the writing of a dream-work.

Wakean humor differs from that found in *Ulysses* because the later work contains no conscious jokers such as Mulligan. In fact, the social teleology of humor, the joker's need for the laughter and endorsement of a listener to achieve pleasure, is not present in the *Wake.* The washerwoman who snaps to her friend, "You'd like the coifs and guimpes, snouty, and me to do the greasy jub on old Veronica's wipers" (204.29), is oblivious to the outrageous comparison between Veronica's veil, bloodied by the imprint of Christ's face, and a woman's menstrual napkin. The humor in *Finnegans Wake* is as unpremeditated and spontaneous as the humor in the dream. Shaun interrupts a critical moment in his interrogation with laughter; when reproved by his inquisitors, he claims to have laughed involuntarily ("I didn't say it aloud, sir. I have something inside of me talking to myself" [522.25]). Freud tells us that the joke is, in fact, involuntary, and that, strictly speaking, we do not know what we are laughing about.[22]

The genesis and rationale of Joycean humor may be traced to the famous discussion of aesthetic theory in *Portrait.* Founding art on a principle of "stasis," Stephen's own elegant exposition exemplifies all the conditions of the classical and rational art he describes. Lynch's responses and comments, in contrast, express the restless cravings of the id, the sexual, the profane. Grossly physical, erratic, excitable, he punctuates Stephen's cool, formal discourse with curses and laughter. Their dialectical discussion resembles a parody of the confrontation of man's higher and lower nature, reason and instinct, angel and demon. In *Finnegans Wake,* this dialectical discussion is condensed into the single line of discourse. The unconscious continually erupts in the humorless discourse, exerting its infantile claim to pleasure in jokes, puns, and double entendres. The speakers of the discourse pass over these outbursts without notice, like Stephen, who either ignores or dismisses Lynch's humorous banter ("As for that, Stephen said in polite parenthesis, we are all animals. I also am an animal. . . . But we are just now in a mental world" [*P,* p. 206]). Stephen is the supreme pompous ass in this scene, and his cold, aristocratic theory of art is subverted by the coarse, proletarian cravings of Lynch. In *Finnegans Wake* these personifications yield to the portrayal of a single self exhibiting these conflicting aspects.

Wit and humor in the dream or in waking life result from the unconscious resistance to the repression of pleasure. The thrust of the dream is wish-fulfillment, Freud tells us, and the unconscious produces puns and comic effects in its attempt to outflank the censor. This causal relationship between repression and wit is best delineated in Freud's theory of errors as presented in "The Psychopathology of Everyday Life" and the *General Introduction.* Many of the errors are hilarious, particularly slips of the pen such as "clown prince" for "crown prince."[23] The error is caused by the repression of the writer's true feelings and their unconscious eruption in the misprint. The humor resides in the incongruity or discrepancy between the two descriptions of the same man—an incongruity existing originally between the honest and hypocritical expressions of the writer.

A comic theme in Joyce's work whose source is a psychological conflict is that of the lecherous instructor. The theme is developed to best effect in the portrait of Jaun before the girls of St. Bride's, where the severity of the moral injunction fails to hide the prurient interest of this preacher ("asking coy one after sloy one had she read Irish legginds and gently reproving one that the ham of her hom could be seen below her hem and whispering another aside, as lavariant, that the hook of her hum was open a bittock at her back" [431.4]). Shem indulges a similar fantasy, imagining he would be a good tutor to Issy, "turning up and fingering over the most dantellising peaches in the lingerous longerous book of the dark" (251.23). Perhaps Shem is only thinking of turning up and fingering the most tantalizing pages of the Egyptian

Book of the Dead, or perhaps, as Campbell and Robinson suggest,[24] he desires, like Dante's Paolo, to seduce a Francesca with a love story in a book, perhaps the *Inferno* itself. But tantalizing peaches, besides whatever *ad hoc* sexual images they conjure up, are the two young girls pursued by the old geezer in an earlier version of the Phoenix Park sin (65.26), and Shem's "turning up and fingering over" sounds far from innocent.

Without the element of conflict, the theme of the lecher or the instructor, which occurs in Joyce's early fiction, loses its humor. Mr. Duffy in "A Painful Case," for example, becomes Mrs. Sinico's instructor ("He lent her books, provided her with ideas, shared his intellectual life with her" [*D*, p. 110]). But Mr. Duffy's sexual repression is so complete that he recoils from the smallest demonstration of affection. Conversely, a confirmed seducer like Corley in "Two Gallants" never represses his shabby desires at all.

Yet conflict itself is not enough to produce humor. In the preacher Davidson of Somerset Maugham's "Rain," repressed sexual desires erupt like a volcano as he rapes the prostitute he has converted. The ironic incongruity of conflicting impulses existing side by side is sacrificed in favor of showing Davidson's destruction by the extremes of his nature. The humor that could have resulted from the successful victory over repression is blocked by the ultimate triumph of Davidson's superego, which drives him to suicide.

The reverse of the theme of instruction/seduction is the theme of academic/sexual learning. While the young narrator of "The Encounter" discovers homosexual sadism while playing hookey, young Stephen Dedalus learns of it right there at Clongowes, at school. By the time he elaborates the relationship between scientific and erotic knowledge in the lesson chapter (II.2) of *Finnegans Wake,* Joyce shifts the object of curiosity from the peripheral perversities of the schoolboy to the oedipal heart of the matter. At the same time, the fright that the little boys in the early works receive from their new knowledge is supplanted by a humor born of incongruity and economy. In the lesson chapter it is the academic studies themselves, not truant adventure or playground gossip, that disclose the sexual secrets of the parents to the young boys. As the subjects become drier and more abstract, the sexual knowledge becomes juicier and more blatant, until a geometric diagram reveals the mother's pudendum ("the whome of your eternal geomater" [296.31]). The Freudian justification for the link between scientific and sexual curiosity is concisely stated in a footnote in the *Skeleton Key*.[25]

The lesson chapter (II.2) owes much to the jokes and puns of Lewis Carroll's *Alice in Wonderland.* But while Carroll's "fishy education" is finally an arbitrary one-joke gimmick—"Fainting in Coils" having little to do with Painting in Oils[26]—Joyce's inventions seem logical by comparison. For example, the grammar lesson, conducted by a wise and experienced grandma, properly concerns relationships since the discipline has traditionally encompassed both the arrangement and function of words in a sentence as well as linguistic etiquette. But while "gramma" advises the young girls about first, second, and third persons, masculine, "mascarine," feminine, "phelinine," and neuter, "nuder" (268.17), she herself confuses the cases utterly as she tells of "when him was me hedon and mine . . . his analectual pygmyhop" (268.26) (Anna Livia Plurabelle; analectual: composed of fragments, "pygmyhop": small, doll-like, therefore a rag doll; intellectual pick-me-up?). Other bits of grammatical jargon come to life as they enact their literal meanings ("dative" and "oblative" [268.22] refer to grandpa's comings and goings, "even if obsolete, it is always of interest" adds "gramma" philosophically; "tense accusatives" become emotional and dramatic without strict reference to time and inflections; "all them fine clauses in Lindley's and Murrey's never braught the participle of a present to a desponent hortatrixy" [269.29] turn Lindley and Murray's grammar into a law partnership whose legal "clauses" yield no benefits to the sad defendant, a young female gardener or a downcast whore). This section owes its wit not only to incongruity and economy, but also to a final plausibility, a recognition that with the barest flick of the imagination, a grammar lesson could indeed turn into a lively narrative of persons, cases, and moods.

The style of *Finnegans Wake* is often compared to those visual art forms whose glory lies in a luxuriance of ornamentation—the baroque, rococo, and arabesque. Tindall writes, "It seems an arabesque—the elaborate decoration of something so simple that it evades us. This simple text, like that on some pages of the *Book of Kells,* is lost in the design."[27] I would argue that there is no such "simple text" in *Finnegans Wake.* Insofar as literature must proceed from the human mind, the complexities of *Wake* language are highly functional in representing the dreaming state. They show the work of the dreamer as he constructs and observes the incredible artifact of his dream. Like the builders in the *Wake,* he builds, using thoughts, images, words, memories, and sounds. He sorts through his repertoire of words, pairs some that sound alike, and places some next to others because their context is similar. Sometimes he hides an important idea under a trivial one, or buries an idea beneath such a heap of associations that he must later trace his way through them like Theseus winding the clue ball through the labyrinth. He can move backward and forward in time, be in two places at once, disguise others, and disguise even himself so that he cannot recognize himself. He indulges in a sophisticated kind of play, which resembles nothing so much as the work/play of the poet, and has the same purpose—to communicate and to be understood.

Whatever beauty there is in the style of *Finnegans Wake* lies not in the ornate surfaces or the embellishments. It lies rather in the interstices between words and ideas, in the intricate and devious connections between things, and in the infinite details, carefully sorted and grouped according to the demands of some inarticulate psychic need.

There is something a little inhuman about *Finnegans Wake,* Compared to, say, *Ulysses.* Perhaps this is merely because it is strange, as dreams are strange and alien—so much so that for centuries they were regarded as messages from another, a supernatural or inhuman other. Dreams are poems written in sleep by an unknown other self. Their puzzling quality comes from feelings heavily "defended," to use the psychoanalytic term. *Finnegans Wake* resembles a later genre of films that also defies journalistic curiosity—what Norman Holland calls the "puzzling movies" of the late fifties and sixties. It is closer, in style, if not in content, to Bergman's *Wild Strawberries,* to Fellini's *8½,* or to Resnais's *Last Year at Marienbad,* than to *Ulysses* itself.

6

TECHNIQUE

DECONSTRUCTION

When Samuel Beckett wrote of *Work in Progress,* "Here form *is* content, content *is* form,"[1] he seemed to beg the same question that Yeats so wisely left in rhetorical form at the end of "Among School-children." Beckett goes on to support his comment by noting, "His writing is not *about* something; *it is that something itself.* . . . When the sense is sleep, the words go to sleep. . . . When the sense is dancing, the words dance." True, of course, but the same could be said even more convincingly about *Ulysses,* particularly the *tour de force* of "Oxen in the Sun," and the musical form of "Sirens." Questions of content and form in *Finnegans Wake* must at least explain its difference from *Ulysses,* and this difference is quite simple. Whatever its mythical underpinnings, *Ulysses* is about three people, Stephen Dedalus, Leopold Bloom, and Molly Bloom, in Dublin, Ireland on 16 June 1904. On Bloomsday, every 16 June, we can take Bloomsday pilgrimages in Dublin because we know exactly where Bloom spent his entire day. In fact, we know Bloom as well as we are ever likely to know any fictional character. On the other hand, Nathan Halper notwithstanding, we don't know when Earwicker dreams, or if he dreams, or if his name is really Humphrey (it could be Harold) Chimpden Earwicker (it could be Porter or Coppinger or O'Reilly). We know that Molly is voluptuous, but

Earwicker's hunchback, for all we know, could merely be that suspicious parcel he is sometimes reported to be toting around. The major difference between *Ulysses* and *Finnegans Wake* is clearly that in *Ulysses* we can be certain of most things, whereas in *Finnegans Wake* we must be uncertain. The greatest critical mistake in approaching *Finnegans Wake* has been the assumption that we can be certain of who, where, and when everything is in the *Wake,* if only we do enough research. The discovery that Maggie is ALP may be true enough, but it doesn't mean anything. ALP is also Kate, the old slopwoman, and Isabel, the daughter, and Biddie Doran, the hen, in a way that Molly Bloom is decidedly *not* Mrs. Riordan, or Milly, or Josie Breen.

In the course of several chapters, I have examined this lack of certainty in every aspect of the work. Events in *Finnegans Wake* repeat themselves as compulsively as Scheherazade did, spinning her tales, until there are so many versions of the event that one can no longer discover the "true" one. Wakean events can reverse themselves so that we do not know if father seduces daughter or daughter tempts father. The Wakean family is therefore in chaos because, through incest and parricide, family roles and family relationships are violated in such a way that figures can no longer be defined. Consequently identities are unstable and interchangeable, and the self is constantly alienated from itself and fails to know itself. This self-alienation is manifested in a language which is devious, which conceals and reveals secrets, and therefore, like poetry, uses words and images that can mean several, often contradictory, things at once.

The formal elements of the work, plot, character, point of view, and language, are not anchored to a single point of reference, that is, they do not refer back to a center. This condition produces that curious flux and restlessness in the work, which is sensed intuitively by the reader and which the *Wake* itself describes as follows.

Every person, place and thing in the chaosmos of Alle anyway connected with the gobblydumped turkery was moving and changing every part of the time: the travelling inkhorn (possibly pot), the hare and turtle pen and paper, the continually more and less intermisunderstanding minds of the anticollaborators, the as time went on as it will variously inflected, differently pronounced, otherwise spelled, changeably meaning vocable scriptsigns. (118.21)

The substitutability of parts for one another, the variability and uncertainty of the work's structural and thematic elements, represent a decentered universe, one that lacks the center that defines, gives meaning, designates, and holds the structure together—by holding it in immobility. Samuel Beckett acknowledges this when he calls the book a purgatorial work for its lack of any Absolute.[2]

The literary heterodoxy of *Finnegans Wake* is the result of Joyce's attack on the traditional concept of structure itself. This attack was not isolated, but belonged to an "event" or "rupture" in the history of the concept of structure, which, according to philosopher Jacques Derrida, took place in the history of thought sometime in the late nineteenth and early twentieth centuries. The destructive impact of this "event" becomes clear only in view of the history of metaphysics, which Derrida characterizes as belief in being as "presence." "The whole history of the concept of structure, before the rupture I spoke of, must be thought of as a series of substitutions of center for center, as a linked chain of determinations of the center."[3]

A clear illustration of this historic concept of structure can be found in T. E. Hulme's influential work, *Speculations.* Hulme evaluated Classicism and Romanticism, whose dialectics he regarded as forming the basis of the history of art, in terms of a single fundamental premise: that belief in a Deity constitutes the fixed part of man's nature.[4] Hulme denounced Romanticism as the displacement of that fixed belief in Deity from the religious sphere, to which it properly belongs, to the human sphere, that is, the belief in man as a god. Fundamental to Hulme's tenets is, therefore, the notion of a center according to which man defines himself; the issue is merely who or what shall occupy that center.

The "rupture" in the history of structure—brought about, as Derrida says, by our being self-consciously forced to "think the structurality of structure"—results in the idea of a structure in which presence is not so much absent as unlocatable. The center is ex-centric, and the structure is determined not by presence but by play. This "rupture" is manifested most purely in certain destructive discourses of the early twentieth century.

Where and how does this decentering, this notion of the structurality of structure, occur? ... I would probably cite the Nietzschean critique of metaphysics, the critique of the concepts of being and truth, for which were substituted the concepts of play, interpretation, and sign (sign without truth present); the Freudian critique of self-presence, that is, the critique of consciousness, of the subject, of self-identity and of self-proximity or self-possession; and, more radically, the Heideggerean destruction of metaphysics, of onto-theology, of the determination of being as presence.[5]

   Among these destructive discourses of the early twentieth century, *Finnegans Wake* served as a literary exemplar, and in doing so inaugurated a new concept of literary structure, which itself could not be deciphered so long as critical formalism was ruled by concepts like Hulme's.

   As an artist deeply concerned with the philosophical implications of the creative process, Joyce must have faced the special difficulties of trying to create something truly "new" in his last work. He was clearly aware of a problem whose linguistic and anthropological implications are of great interest at the present time: that the *Weltanschauung* of a writer is limited by the language he employs. The image of Shem writing with his own shit on his own body about himself indicates not only the scatological and solipsistic nature of the creative act, but also the entrapment in what is apparently a closed system. The writer who tries to escape the epistemology of his culture is confronted by a language embedded with inherited concepts; to criticize these concepts he must still make use of a language in which they are embedded. Jacques Derrida writes, "It is a question of putting expressly and systematically the problem of the status of a discourse which borrows from a heritage the resources necessary for the deconstruction of that heritage itself."[6] In other words, a "new" literary vision that seeks to critique previous literary modes must use the tools of those same modes—language, concepts, themes, conventions—in the process of the critique itself. William Carlos Williams describes this frustration in *Spring and All,* where the artist imaginatively annihilates the universe to create it anew, only to discover that "EVOLUTION HAS REPEATED ITSELF FROM THE BEGINNING. . . . In fact now, for the first time, everything IS new. . . . The terms 'veracity', 'actuality', 'real', 'natural', 'sincere' are being discussed at length, every word in the discussion being evolved from an identical discussion which took place the day before yesterday."[7] To outflank this contradiction, Joyce needed to decenter the literary structure, a process that would affect every aspect of the work so radically as to make it unique in literary history. The traditional concept of structure, which implied a center or presence, also implied a formal wholeness of the work of art, in which each of the particular elements referred always back to the center. Decentering of the structure, then, suggests another, as yet uncategorizable sense of form—which modern poets often call "open" in contrast to "closed," but which is more conveniently defined here as "freeplay." Jacques Derrida describes this freeplay of a decentered system of language as follows. "This field is in fact that of *freeplay,* that is to say, a field of infinite substitutions in the closure of a finite ensemble. This field permits these infinite substitutions only because it is finite, that is to say, because instead of being an inexhaustible field, as in the classical hypothesis, instead of being too large, there is something missing from it: a center which arrests and founds the freeplay of substitutions."[8] The freeplay of elements in *Finnegans Wake* has long been recognized without pursuit of its implications for the total structure of the work. William York Tindall writes, "As God's world, created by the Word, is an endless arrangement and rearrangement of ninety-six elements—give or take a couple—so Joyce's closed system is an endless arrangement and rearrangement of a thousand and one elements that, whatever their multiplicity, are limited in number."[9]

It is freeplay that makes characters, times, places, and actions interchangeable in *Finnegans Wake,* that breaks down the all-important distinction between the self and the other, and that makes uncertainty a governing principle of the work. In order to effect this "new" decentered literary structure and to implement freeplay not only in the themes of the work but in the language as well, Joyce instituted two major techniques: a new application of "imitative form," and a building technique I will call *bricolage,* borrowing a term from anthropologist Lévi-Strauss.

IMITATIVE FORM

Finnegans Wake includes those imitative techniques so successfully employed in *Ulysses:* the imitation of printed formats as in "Aeolus" and the "Triv and Quad" chapter (II.2), the imitation of sounds in "Sirens" and "Anna Livia Plurabelle" (I.8), and the imitation of pedagogical modes as in the catechism of "Eumaeus" and the quiz show of I.6. But the *Wake* language far surpasses the experiments of *Ulysses* as a type of verbal simulation. The stylistic incorporation of the novel's themes depends on the most fundamental correspondence between social and linguistic structures. The law of man and the law of language are homologous systems because they share an identical unconscious structure. The father's symbolic function as figure of the law is therefore analogous to the semantic function of language, which assigns to lexical items their meanings and their grammatical functions. The primordial law of the father, the incest taboo and the kinship regulations, function like those laws of phonological combination which permit certain sounds to be combined only in certain ways in the formation of words, and those laws of syntax that regulate the relationships of words in the formation of the sentence.[10] That the theme of the fallen father, the fallen God, has linguistic repercussions is suggested in the *Wake* itself ("Gwds with gurs are gttrdmmrng. Hlls vlls. The timid hearts of words all exeomnosunt" [258.1]). The vowels are here the "timid hearts of words" which flee with the defeated gods: the words can no longer be spoken, like many of the words in the *Wake,* and their meaning becomes dislocated, uncertain. The familial/linguistic correspondence is also revealed in the passage that describes the shooting of the Russian General, a type of parricide (*"The abnihilisation of the etym by the grisning of the grosning of the grinder of the grunder of the first lord of Hurtreford expolodotonates through Parsuralia with an ivanmorinthorrorumble fragoromboassity amidwhiches general uttermosts confussion are perceivable moletons skaping with mulicules"* [353.22]). The "etym," or word, is also "etymon," which, as the primary word from which a derivative is formed, corresponds to father. Although the construction of the phrase, "abnihilisation of the etym," is essentially ambiguous—it is not clear whether "etym" is the subject or object of the action implied in abnihilisation, or a creation out of nothing—the implication is that in either case, the fall of the father creates first of all noise, an "ivanmorinthorrorumble fragoromboassity." The equation of word and void occurs also in a parody of St. John's gospel prologue in II.2 ("In the buginning is the woid, in the muddle is the sounddance and thereinofter you're in the unbewised again" [378.29]). If the father signifies the semantic function of language, the act of giving names to things or assigning meanings to words, then the fall of the father in *Finnegans Wake* signifies that severing of words from their referents which creates a linguistic freeplay, a "sound-dance," or "variously inflected, differently pronounced, otherwise spelled, changeably meaning vocable scriptsigns" (118.26), and therefore one is clearly in the "unbewised," the unproven (German: *Beweis*), the uncertain, again. Hugh Kenner, after quoting a sentence from the *Wake,* remarks, "It is worse than useless to push this toward one or the other of the meanings between which it hangs; to paraphrase it, for instance, in terms of porter being uncorked and poured. It is equally misleading to scan early drafts for the author's intentions, on the assumption that a 'meaning' got buried by elaboration. Joyce worked seventeen years to push the work away from 'meaning,' adrift into language; nothing is to be gained by trying to push it back."[11]

If the ultimate meaningful word is the theological Logos, the Word of John's prologue, then its antithesis might be Stephen's recurrent notion in *Ulysses* ("God: noise in the street" [*U*, p. 186]). The fall of the father, which marks the disjunction of word from meaning, results in noise, as the *Wake* passage cited earlier seems to suggest. The *Wake* repeats Stephen's concept of God as a noise in the street and amplifies it to thematic proportions. At the end of II.1, there appears a litany which includes the invocation, "Loud, hear us!/Loud, graciously hear us!" (258.25). The substitution of "Loud" for "Lord" is, of course, consistent with the Wakean proposition that the voice of God, the voice of the father, is the sound of thunder, and that the thunder announces the father's fall (cf. 3.15). Other associations of the father's fall with noise include reference to the tower of Babel: the fallen giant MacCool, marking with his body the geography of Dublin, is described as an "overgrown babeling" (6.31), a fallen tower of Babel or babbling baby. Both babble, the first speech of the infant man, and thunder, the first word of God to postlapsarian man, represent sound without meaning or signification.

The events of *Finnegans Wake* are steeped in noise: the crash of falling towers, bridges, men, Wall Street, and civilizations; the clamor of countless battles; the boisterous happenings in Earwicker's pub; the angry invectives of quarreling antagonists. As someone says in the midst of the drunken shouting and raucous merrymaking at Finn MacCool's wake, "E'erawhere in this whorl would ye hear sich a din again?" (6.24). Furthermore, the gossip, rumor, and slander discussed in the previous section illustrate an archaic definition of the word "noise" as "common talk, rumor, evil report, or scandal"—a definition that still survives in the dual meaning of the word "report." In its perfect fusion of noise and rumor, *Finnegans Wake* resembles nothing so much as Chaucer's *The House of Fame*.

The noise that characterizes the thematic events of *Finnegans Wake* is expressed stylistically by a number of technical devices. There are many "voices" in the *Wake*—numerous utterances by the various figures, frequently unidentified, and often seeming to occur all at once, like many people shouting and clamoring simultaneously ("Mulo Mulelo! Homo Humilo! Dauncy a deady O! Dood dood dood! O Bawse! O Boese! O Muerther! O Mord! . . . Malawinga! Malawunga! Ser Oh Ser! See ah See! Hamovs! Hemoves! Mamor!" [499.5]) In addition, any given utterance can be considered to contain a number of voices, as Clive Hart notes, "In theory, highly controlled choral speaking by a small group would be the only satisfactory solution to the problem of how to read *Finnegans Wake* aloud, each speaker adhering to one 'voice' of the counterpoint and using the appropriate accent and stress."[12] Stylistically, however, the *Wake* not only simulates the sound of "noise," as in the onomatopoeic thunder, but the concept of noise as an obstruction to the understanding of a message, as well. As a principle of information theory, noise is any interference in the transmission of information. "Whatever medium is used for the purpose of transmitting information, it will be subject to various unpredictable physical disturbances, which will obliterate or distort part of the message and thus lead to the loss of information. If the system were free of redundancy, the information lost would be irrecoverable."[13] If we grant that little information is transmitted to the reader of *Finnegans Wake* even when we disregard the interference generated by the labyrinthian progress of the narrative or the interference inherent in the linguistic distortions, another rationale for the work's length and extraordinary redundancy becomes apparent. Joyce clearly followed a sound principle of information theory in *Finnegans Wake:* a work with an unprecedented amount of "interference" requires an unprecedented amount of seemingly gratuitous repetition in compensation.

The familial/linguistic homology can be most simply illustrated with reference to simple grammatical slot and filler technique. The family consists of certain slots or positions which are occupied by certain individuals—for example, slot F (father) is occupied by HCE, slot M (mother), by ALP, slot D (daughter), by Isabel. The incest taboo decrees that slot M can be filled by any woman except Isabel, the daughter, HCE's mother or sister, and so on. The laws that govern the combinations of sounds in words, or words in sentences, work in a similar manner. In the potential English word "_lan" for example, the initial slot cannot be filled by the sounds of "m," "n," "d," "t," "r," or "v." In the sentence "The____told us," the slot may *not* be filled by another article like "a" or "an," a preposition like "into" or "from," a pronoun like "she," or even a proper noun like "George." In other words, the social structure of the family and the linguistic structure of the sentence is intelligible only if certain laws of combination are observed. The theme of incest in *Finnegans Wake* is stylistically simulated in a language that violates linguistic laws of combination, that is, phonotactic or syntactic laws.

While the rules of permissible phonological combinations must account for all the actual words in the English lexicon, they also encompass words that are not, in fact, actualized in the language, but could be without violating these rules. John Lyons notes some interesting applications of these "potential" words.

> Many of the non-occurrent combinations of phonemes would be accepted by native speakers as more 'normal' than others; they are, not only easily pronounceable, but in some way similar in form to other words of the language. . . . It is noticeable, for instance, and it has often been pointed out, that writers of nonsense verse (like Lewis Carroll or Edward Lear) will create 'words' which almost invariably conform to the phonological structure of actual words in the language; and the same is true of brand-names invented for manufactured products.[14]

The bulk of Joyce's "nonsense" words in the *Wake* are such potential English words: "flosting" (501.33) and "marracks" (15.36), for example. In many words, however, the combination of sounds is quite impossible in English: "tuvavnr" (54.15), "dgiaour" (68.18), "stlongfella" (82.13), "trwth" (132.5), "tsifengtse" (299.26), "remoltked" (333.13), or "grianblachk" (503.23).

The task confronting Joyce in letting the language reflect a universe whose structure is determined by substitutions and freeplay, is to deconstruct the language itself. Of course, this involves the paradox of critical language, the need to use language to represent the deconstruction of language. One of the strategies Joyce uses to communicate a deconstructed language involves his interesting manipulation of structure words. Structure words—articles, prepositions, auxiliaries, intensifiers, and the like—have essentially no semantic content but act like the mortar that holds the lexical bricks of the sentence in place. Sometimes Joyce substitutes descriptive words for these structural items as in "How wooden I not know it" (16.33) and "you skull see" (17.18), where "wooden" and "skull" replace "wouldn't" and "shall" in the auxiliary slots in the sentence. The *Wake* sentences are now ungrammatical, but they still communicate because the reader unconsciously recognizes the slot and knows the correct filler. Such substitutions also occur frequently in cases not involving structure words. For example, the items "who eight the last of the goosebellies" (142.2) and "were we bread by the same fire" (168.8), show questionable substitutions in slots that are usually occupied by verbs.

Besides filling linguistic slots with impermissible fillers, Joyce further disrupts linguistic structure by ignoring internal junctures. Internal junctures, the meaningful pauses between words, are treated as suprasegmental phonemes in modern linguistics because they function to distinguish the meanings of otherwise identical units, as for example the joke in W. C. Fields's *The Dentist,* where there is confusing talk of either "an ice man" or "a nice man." In the *Wake* we find such expressions as "an earsighted view" (143.9) and "the course of his tory" (143.12)—irregular expressions produced by incorrect junctures. Joyce also used junctures to perform such interesting substitutions as "to be cause" (16.18), "dumptied the wholeborrow of rubbages on to soil here" (17.4), and "they are in surgence" (17.25). He clearly realized that many prefixes sound like prepositions. So the "be" of "because" becomes a verb on the order of "to be sure"; the "to" of "onto" becomes an infinitive that changes "soil" from a noun to a verb; and the prefix "in" of "insurgence" becomes a preposition that changes the meaning of "are" from "may be identified with" to "are located."

Violations of junctures also produce other interesting linguistic aberrations. The expression, "how he stud theirs" (234.10), probably derives from an artificial juncture in the resonant "how he stutters." "As bold and as madhouse a bull in a meadows" (353.13) ignores the junction between "mad as" to create "madhouse." An interesting case of overlap occurs in the expression, "pleasekindly communicake with the original sinse we are only yearning" (239.1), where the juncture can come either before or after "sinse" depending on whether it is read as "sins" or as "since." These examples demonstrate how syntactic disruption produces the uncertainty and ambiguity that must characterize a decentered language.

Joyce introduces ungrammaticality into *Finnegans Wake* deliberately. The expression, "after having said your poetry," is quite all right, while "after having sat your poetries" (435.26) is ungrammatical because "sat" is an obligatory intransitive and cannot take a direct object. To return to the correspondence between social and linguistic structures in *Finnegans Wake,* we can charge much of the thematic confusion and ambiguity to a kind of ungrammaticality. For example, a very common basic sentence pattern, illustrated as "____kills____" shows the importance of syntactic structure. When Alice reads the nonsense poem "Jabberwocky" in *Alice in Wonderland,* she knows, without understanding all the words, "*somebody* killed *something*: that's clear, at any rate."[15] Yet it is precisely these crucial relations between subjects and objects that are often deliberately ambiguous in *Finnegans Wake.* As with Oedipus and Laius, father-son enmity is complex and Laius tries to kill Oedipus as surely as Oedipus does kill him. So in *Finnegans Wake,* there is enough confusion to have to ask "who struck Buckley though nowadays as thentimes every school-filly . . . knows as yayas is yayas how it was Buckleyself . . . struck and the Russian generals, da! da!, instead of Buckley who was caddishly struck by him when be herselves" (101.15). The many reversible actions in *Finnegans Wake* serve precisely to make distinctions between subjects and objects difficult. The questions that surround the sin in Phoenix Park are reduced continually to this kind of ambiguity: Did HCE seduce the girls or did the girls tempt HCE? Did HCE watch the girls urinate or did the girls watch HCE deliberately expose himself? Did ALP start the wars and deluge that mark the collapse of civilization, or did she merely clean up the rubbish afterwards? Did Shem forge the Letter or did Shaun steal the Letter from Shem? The subject/object confusions are types of thematic ambiguity that approximate the syntactic ambiguity of the language.

Joyce's inclusion of multitudinous fragments of foreign languages in the *Wake* is also consistent with the principle of freeplay. Unlike artificial or "auxiliary" languages whose purpose is to overcome the Babelian diversity of national languages, Joyce's "muttering pot" (20.7) in the *Wake* appears to be a dump or rubbish heap like ALP's scavenger sack, in which the fragments merely mix and mingle to be distributed anew. Citing examples, Ronald Buckalew notes, "Joyce's foreign language is often distorted and mixed to produce puns and jokes."[16] The mixing of various languages in the same work may represent a type of linguistic miscegenation that imitates the thematic incest. The parallel is not inappropriate, particularly since we speak of the historical development of languages in terms of the relationships of language "families."

Joyce once wrote of *Finnegans Wake,* "What the language will look like when I have finished I don't know. But having declared war I shall go on *jusqu'au bout.*"[17]   If Joyce violates the laws of language, he does no more than to adapt the language to a vision in which law has been supplanted by play—a linguistic freeplay that is the fertile ground for new semantic and syntactic forms, for a thoroughgoing linguistic originality.

BRICOLAGE

Richard Ellmann aptly describes *Finnegans Wake* as "a wholly new book based upon the premise that there is nothing new under the sun."[18] This paradox is clearly the crux of the philosophical problem that Joyce set out to solve technically in *Finnegans Wake.* Hart and Atherton attribute Joyce's artistic dependence on the inherited matter of the cultural and personal past to a sense of religious prohibition, a guilt which Joyce associated with the creative process. However, judging from the profanity which, no doubt, qualifies *Finnegans Wake* as one of the most aggressively sacrilegious books in the language, the notion of Joyce's fearing "the presumption of human attempts at creation"[19] is untenable.

More plausibly, Joyce realized that he could not escape his debt to the culture, the language, and the literature. The well-known works on comparative mythology, which so influenced Eliot and Yeats, impressed Joyce also with the persistence of mythic structures, as we know from *Ulysses.* The artist has no choice but to plunder his heritage, and Joyce, at least, acknowledges the debt grandly, calling *Finnegans Wake* an "epical forged cheque" (181.16) and "the last word in stolentelling" (424.35).

To confront this dilemma, Joyce resorts to a technical method which critics have already identified in their comparisons of *Finnegans Wake* to the "objet trouvé" collage. "Bits and pieces are picked up and incorporated into the texture with little modification, while the precise nature of each individual fragment is not always of great importance."[20] Borrowing a term which Lévi-Strauss applies to mythical thought and mythological activity in *The Savage Mind,* this practice of using bits and pieces of heterogeneous materials without regard to their specific function, may be called *bricolage.* Joyce once asked his Aunt Josephine, send "any news you like, programmes, pawntickets, press cuttings, handbills. I like reading them."[21] Joyce is like Lévi-Strauss's *bricoleur,* collecting and saving things "on the principle that 'they may always come in handy.' "[22] That Joyce's method certainly approximated that of the *bricoleur* is most evident in his voluminous working notebooks for the *Wake,* crammed as these are with list upon list of apparently unrelated words, phrases, snatches of thought, and bits of data.[23]

More important than Joyce's writing practice, however, is the way in which this method, *bricolage,* allows Joyce to liberate materials from their old contexts, to juxtapose them freely, and allow them to enter into new and unexpected combinations with each other. Lévi-Strauss writes of the *bricoleur,* "Now, the characteristic feature of mythical thought, as of 'bricolage' on the practical plane, is that it builds up structured sets, not directly with other structured sets but by using the remains and debris of events: in French 'des bribes et des morceaux,' or odds and ends in English, fossilized evidence of the history of an individual or a society."[24]

Some of Joyce's puns and verbal jokes demonstrate this technique of salvaging bits and pieces for new purposes and uses. In *Ulysses,* the pornographic *Ruby, the Pride of the Ring* becomes a ruby ring which Bloom slips romantically on Josie Breen's finger during the Nighttown hallucinations (*U,* p. 445). Our understanding of Joyce's use of the battle of Waterloo in the *Wake* will be little improved by checking up on facts in a history book. In *bricoleur* fashion, Joyce uses the event as it comes to hand, and what seems to interest him chiefly is the word-play potential which makes the battleground the site of urinating girls. The Crash of Wall Street resulted in the Great Depression, and if it is a giant or an egg that falls from the wall, then the economic disaster of the thirties becomes merely an enormous imprint of the fallen giant's body on the topography of Dublin.

Finnegans Wake is unmistakably original—and just as self-consciously unoriginal. In its bizarre, distorted language are lodged all of Joyce's immense, but thoroughly familiar, preoccupations: the Dublin of his youth, familial relationships, sexual obsessions, bits of military and political history, allusions to a multitude of literary works, sacred books, arcane writings, old myths, fables, fairy tales, children's games, songs, riddles, and great quantities of talk. But his technique of taking bits and pieces of the old and using them to create something new is, perhaps, best illustrated by showing how various themes and motifs from the early works take on new life in *Finnegans Wake.* Joyce's earliest known fiction attempts, a story intended for *Tidbits* and a sketch from *Silhouettes,* both remembered by Stanislaus, reappear in the *Wake.* The *Tidbit* story is recounted as follows. "In it a man who has attended a masked ball dressed as a prominent Russian diplomat is walking by the Russian Embassy on his way home, thinking about the 'laughing witch,' his fiancée, when a Nihilist tries to assassinate him. The police arrest him as well as his assailant, but his fiancée, hearing of the attempt, realizes what has happened and comes to the police station to explain and release him."[25] The incident reflects the many versions of the encounter with the assailant that recur throughout *Finnegans Wake*—for example, the HCE-cad encounter and Buckley's shooting of the Russian General. It includes all the usual elements: the oedipal case of mistaken identity, the arrival of the constable, and the woman as temptress and redeemer of the fallen man.

Stanislaus describes the scene from *Silhouettes* as "two figures in violent agitation on a lowered window blind illuminated from within, the burly figure of a man, staggering and threatening with upraised fist, and the smaller sharp-faced figure of a nagging woman."[26] A similar scene is reenacted in the dumbshow of III.4, where the couple is described as "Man looking round, beastly expression ... exhibits rage. . . . Woman, sitting . . . haggish expression, peaky nose . . . exhibits fear" (559.22). In the same chapter, the voyeurism of the narrator watching the illuminated blind becomes explicit when the couple's copulation is flashed in silhouette on the screen of the blind.

Dubliners is filled with images of the fallen father, a collection of family men in various stages of brutalization and Dublin paralysis. Once drunk, they threaten their small children like the anonymous man in the *Silhouettes* story. Eveline's father rudely invades the children's games, brandishing his blackthorn stick, much like the father (II.1) in *Finnegans Wake* ("Housefather calls enthreateningly ... In thundercloud periwig. With lightning bug aflash from afinger" [246.6]). Insofar as the children's games are social and sexual in nature, the threatening father who calls the children home is Vico's thunder, which frightened the copulating couples into taking shelter in the caves and which they interpreted as the voice of a commanding God. Joyce once wrote to Harriet Shaw Weaver, "Children may just as well play as not. The ogre will come in any case."[27]

Other frightening fathers in *Dubliners* include the hard-drinking, brutal Farrington of "Counterparts," and Little Chandler, who in parody of Farrington merely drinks a few exceptional whiskeys on a special occasion and then, shockingly, shouts at his infant. ALP, like Chandler's wife, soothes her child who is frightened by "thunner in the eire" (565.17). He is only dreaming, she tells him, and frightened of phantoms ("No bad bold faathern, dear one" [565.19]).

A *Dubliner* precurser of the *Wake*'s Tim Finnegan image is Tom Kernan in "Grace," who falls down the steps of the bar while drunk. A constable comes and he is taken home and put to bed. Next day, his friends gather round the bed and, amid bottles of stout, urge Kernan to renew himself spiritually through a religious retreat. Joyce uses a similar version of this incident to recapitulate the Tim Finnegan/Finn Mac-Cool wake of I.1 later in the book when the publican falls drunkenly to the floor and stumbles up to bed for renewal in sleep and dream. The incident involving the drunken Stephen and the two soldiers at the end of *Ulysses* follows the same pattern. However, in addition to the theme of the fall of the drunken man, Stephen's incident includes an HCE-like quarrel with the soldiers over the whores. "Up, guards, and at them!" (*U*, p. 596), yells Major Tweedy in "Circe," a refrain that reverber-ates throughout *Finnegans Wake*. Furthermore, all the suspicion of buggery surrounding the involvement of HCE and the three soldiers "When some bugger let down the backtrap of the omnibus/and he caught his death of fusiliers" [47.9]) may be a literal animation of the bawdy expressions of Privates Carr and Compton, "Here bugger off, Harry" (*U* p. 602) or "God fuck old Bennett! He's a whitearsed bugger" (*U*, p. 603). The "whitearsed" bugger may also be a source for Wellington's white horse which, covered with Napoleon's hat, is blown or shot "off of the top of the tail on the back of his big wide harse. Tip (Bullseye! Game!)" (10.19), like a target on a pinball machine, or the Russian General, or buggered HCE himself.

The image of melancholy men in "Ivy Day in the Committee Room" reminiscing about Parnell, or the Dedalus family discussing the old scandal at Christmas dinner, recurs in similar patterns in *Finnegans Wake*. The pub customers of II.3 discuss several affairs, including the Norwegian captain story and the Butt/Taff skit, while drinking heartily. The sorrowful and reverent poem on "The Death of Parnell" (*D*, pp. 134, 135) recurs without reverence or solemnity of either style or spirit as "The Ballad of Persse O'Reilly" in the *Wake* (45.7, 47.26). The poems have many reversed parallels. *"He is dead. Our Uncrowned King is dead"* becomes "He was one time our King of the Castle/Now he's kicked about like a rotten old parsnip." Parnell's lofty ideals ("He dreamed [alas, 'twas but a dream!]/ Of Liberty") give way to HCE's vulgar ones ("We had chaw chaw chops, chairs, chewing gum, the chickenpox and china chambers/ Universally provided by this soffsoaping salesman"). While Parnell's second coming is joyously anticipated ("But Erin, list, his spirit may/Rise, like the Phoenix from the flames") hope of HCE's rebirth is fatalistically and sensibly squelched ("And not all the king's men nor his horses/Will resurrect his corpus").

The themes of games and competition, which express the brother antagonism in the *Wake*, occur in the early works as trials of brawn, as in "Counterparts," and brain, as in "Little Cloud." Games and competition involving nationalism and women are particularly germane to *Finnegans Wake*. The nationalistic implications of the games in "After the Race," prefigure the imperialistic conflicts of the later works, Bloom's encounter with the Cyclops, and the various native-invader quarrels in the *Wake*. Rivalry over women is most prominent in "The Dead," where Gabriel must compete with a dead boy for Gretta's love, and in the jealous triangles in *Exiles, Portrait,* and *Ulysses.* Stephen's quarrel with the soldiers at the end of "Circe" is particularly interesting in this regard, because it involves both nationalism and women—Stephen's insult to the King and his attentions to Cissy Caffrey.

Many figures in *Dubliners* have secrets: Father Flynn, the truants of "An Encounter," the boy of "Araby," Eveline, Mr. Doran of "The Boarding House," and, of course, Gretta Conroy in "The Dead." The coupling of secret and confession in "The Dead" is given an ironic twist in *Ulysses,* where Bloom's secret pleasures, lusts, fears, and regrets are *confessed to himself* in "Circe," to achieve the kind of healing usually reserved for the priestly confessional or the psychoanalytic couch. In *Finnegans Wake* secrets and confessions become combined in a single operation that conceals and reveals—the dream.

The many complicated roles of women in *Finnegans Wake* are adumbrated in Joyce's early works as well. The washerwomen, gossiping about the father's downfall, are prefigured by the two old women at Father Flynn's wake, who, having washed his corpse and laid him out, discuss his failures and his death.

The temptresses are too numerous to mention. They appear first as lovely apparitions to the boyish imagination: Mangan's sister in "Araby," Emma Clery in *Stephen Hero,* and the fair maid in *Chamber Music*—"My love goes lightly, holding up/Her dress with dainty hand" (*CM,* p. 15). Eveline is a particularly interesting temptress because she is identified both with the dying ALP of *Finnegans Wake*,[28] and with Isabel, the daughter, who is the object of competition between father and lover. Eveline's father forbids her to see Frank. Like ALP, Eveline cooks and cares for a man who threatens and abuses her. A drunken father also abuses Gerty MacDowell, who in turn tempts the older Bloom by exposing herself, like the girls in Phoenix Park.

"The Mime of Mick, Nick, and the Maggies" (II.1), deserves a careful comparison with "Nausicaa" in *Ulysses*. In both chapters the children's games at twilight are suspended in ironic conflict between the religious ceremony of evening Benediction and the sexual ceremonies of seduction. Both ceremonies are conducted in the language of gesture. The priest dispensing incense from the swinging censer is mimicked by Gerty waving her perfumed sachet to Bloom. Notwithstanding the abundance of flowers, less pleasing fragrances prevail in *Finnegans Wake*, thanks to Glugg's urination and flatulence ("holding their noises, they insinuate quiet private, Ni, he makes peace in his preaches and play with esteem" [225.5]). Other types of nonverbal communication in the chapters include the semiotics of colors, flowers, clothing, and scents—codes found in Church liturgy, romantic lore, and at the base of children's games and riddles. The baby's game of peek-a-boo is mimed in Gerty's exposing herself to Bloom, an exposure that reminds Bloom of open flowers and Matt Dillon's bevy of daughters, who play charades like Isabel's trooping girls. "Still it was a kind of language between us" (*U*, p. 372), Bloom thinks of their silent exchange.

While Gerty is involved with the older, paternal Bloom, Cissy Caffrey and Edy Boardman are involved with three little boys (like the soldiers of Phoenix Park), Cissy's brothers, Tommy and Jacky Caffrey, who are quarreling twins, and Edy's baby brother. To three flirtatious questions with mildly incestuous overtones, Tommy gives sullen, negative answers.

—Is Cissy your sweetheart?
—Nao, tearful Tommy said.
—Is Edy Boardman your sweetheart? Cissy queried.
—Nao, Tommy said.
—I know, Edy Boardman said . . . Gerty is Tommy's sweetheart.
—Nao, Tommy said on the verge of tears. (*U*, p. 347)

Unlucky Glugg in *Finnegans Wake* (II.1) has a similar experience.

—Haps thee jaoneofergs?

—Nao.
—Haps thee mayjaunties?
—Naohao.
—Haps thee per causes nunsibellies?
—Naohaohao. (233.21)

While Glugg tries to guess the color of flowers and underdrawers, Bloom makes three guesses at Gerty's perfume, one of them being Glugg's correct answer, "What was it? Heliotrope? No, Hyacinth? Hm. Roses, I think" (*U*, p. 374).

The liturgical references shape the Mime chapter, from the initial sign of the cross (222.24) through ceremonies which appear to include reception into the Sodality (235–37), hymnsinging and censer swinging (234.34), the girls "prostitating their selfs" (235.2) before the altar, like novices, and a final prayer, "Loud, hear us!" (258.25)—like Bloom's profane echoes of the Benediction on Sandymount Strand, "O Lord, that little limping devil" (*U*, p. 370), "Lord, I am wet. Devil you are" (*U*, p. 372).

The most surprising transformation of a character from the early works into a Wakean figure occurs in the case of little Maria of *Dubliners'* "Clay," who reappears as ALP in her guise as peacemaker in *Finnegans Wake*. Maria works in a laundry ("She was always sent for when the women quarrelled over their tubs and always succeeded in making peace" [*D*, p. 99]). The bickering washerwomen on the banks of the Liffey may have originated in Maria's laundry. Maria extends her peacemaking efforts to the quarreling brothers Joe and Alphy, but is not as successful as ALP who manages to bring about "reconciled Romas and Reims" (209.25). Maria is "a very, very small person indeed" (*D*, p. 99), like ALP, who is a "Wery, weeny wight" (102.18), "not up to your elb" (207.36) in height. When she laughs, Maria looks like a witch ("the tip of her nose nearly met the top of her chin" [*D*, p. 101]) as does ALP ("Fenny poor hex she must have charred" [208.31]). And Maria, like ALP, is a great bringer of presents, buying penny cakes and plumcake for the Donnelly family, although she loses the plumcake on the way, and although her gifts do not bring about the peace that ALP's scavenged presents create. However, unlike the spin-sterish, prim Maria, little sharp-faced ALP belongs to the genre of exhausted, nagging wives of drunken, brutish husbands. Their respective songs present this contrast nicely. Maria sings, "*I dreamt that I dwelt in marble halls/With vassals and serfs at my side*" (*D*, p. 106). No dweller of marble halls, ALP has "*Sold him her lease of ninenine-ninetee.* . . . Hoo was the C.O.D.?" (102.33). Maria sings, "I had riches too great to count; could boast/Of a high ancestral name," while ALP wails, "We're all up to the years in hues and cribies" (103.5).

When Joyce wanted to write an epic about common, modern man, he took Homer's *Odyssey* and systematically inverted its values and deflated its dimensions. Yet the result was not an anti-epic, nor is Bloom an anti-hero. Joyce had used a structured set to build up another structured set, in the language of Lévi-Strauss. The result was a work with an almost identical structure but a different ambience; *Ulysses* is simply a modern epic.

When Joyce first began *Finnegans Wake,* he sorted out the unused notes from *Ulysses* and exhumed old anecdotes and tales.[29] The materials for the new book were already in existence—unlike *Portrait,* his later works were not autobiographical and we have no fiction about his mature life on the continent. But he used these worn things freely as we can see from his transformation of the sources. As in the dream, where trivial details are invested with important values, Joyce sometimes took the least important details of stories—for example, the quarreling adult brothers, Joe and Alphy, from "Clay," and the fighting child twins, Jacky and Tommy from "Nausicaa,"—removed them from their old contexts, and made them into major configurations in *Finnegans Wake.* Joyce eschewed an established model, a structured set, in favor of using bits and pieces, "a jetsam litterage of convolvuli of times lost or strayed, of lands derelict and of tongues laggin too" (292.15). He wrote to Harriet Shaw Weaver, "The construction is quite different from *Ulysses* where at least the ports of call were known beforehand."[30]

The *bricoleur* does not begin, like the engineer, with a fully conceived project, a detailed model whose actualization depends on the procurement of tools and materials precisely designed for the purposes of the project. The *bricoleur* uses whatever is at hand for his tools and materials, and the result of his labors will never conform exactly to his original aim, which is sketchy at best.[31] As a result, the project of the *bricoleur* proceeds like an organic growth; Joyce often spoke of *Finnegans Wake* as though it had an independent life of its own, as though it achieved its form without his direction or intervention.[32] Perhaps the difference between Joyce's method in *Portrait* and in *Finnegans Wake* can be described by the different meanings that the important word "forge" holds for each work: in *Portrait,* Joyce fashions and tempers his elements into an impeccably designed artifact; in the *Wake,* he uses essentially devious means, compared with those of the artisan, to create an impressively original design, which on closer inspection consists of unaltered and familiar pieces of junk, borrowed or stolen from the smithies of countless others ("The prouts who will invent a writing there ultimately is the poeta, still more learned, who discovered the raiding there originally. That's the point of eschatology our book of kills reaches for now in soandso many counterpoint words. What can't be coded can be decorded if an ear aye sieze what no eye ere grieved for" [482.31]).

Like the *Book of Kells,* which weaves an imaginative graphic text from the pretext of the Gospels, *Finnegans Wake* is woven from a multitude of earlier literatures. Implied in this process is a plunder ("the raiding there originally"), the hoax of Father Prout. The countless modern versions of ancient myths and themes is proof not of the barrenness of the modern imagination, but of the limited vision of human life permitted the artist. A breaking up of the old structures and recombination of the bits and pieces is the only mode of escape. Eliot suggests as much in *The Wasteland* when he writes, "These fragments I have shored against my ruins." William Carlos Williams speaks of it also in relation to Joyce's style in *Work in Progress.* "If to achieve truth we work with words purely, as a writer must, and all the words are dead or beautiful, how then shall we succeed any better than might a philosopher with dead abstractions or their configurations? . . . There must be something new done with the words. Leave beauty out, or, conceivably, one might begin again, one might break them up to let the staleness out of them as Joyce, I think, has done."[33]

The technique of *bricolage* is most striking at the level of words themselves, where it consists of breaking up words and phrases and reassembling them as they come to hand, without regard to their original functions. A phrase like "goat along nose" (413.28) takes the expressions "God alone knows" and "got a long nose" and invests them simultaneously in the words "goat" and "along" which have nothing to do with either of them, but which refer to earlier pasture jargon, "kidding" and "totether." Grammatically the phrase is meaningful only if we picture a goat at the side of a nose—a novel image indeed, God knows, the result of *bricolage.*

As a result of *bricolage,* the reader of *Finnegans Wake* is required to learn to read all over again, both at the word level and at the greater level of myths and themes. In fact, the process of learning to read may be that primitive act suggested in the coding/decoding passage (482.31) as the raiding (reading) there originally, "reading" in the full sense of the German word *lese,* which is both a reading and a gathering. The reader, like the artist and the *bricoleur,* works by putting one thing with another as it comes to hand, like the child who first learns to read ("We are once amore as babes awondering in a wold made fresh where with the hen in the storyaboot we start from scratch" [336.16]).

In constructing a work from its fragments, broken up and considered with an innocent and unbiased eye, Joyce must have learned again what poets may have forgotten, but what contemporary linguists are now teaching: the significance of linguistic structure. The form of the language is learned unconsciously—even young children who have never heard of an "article" know that "the ball" is correct while "ball the" is not. Throughout *Finnegans Wake,* at all levels of construction, Joyce makes structure meaningful, makes it communicate quite independently of content. Therefore, it is fitting that Joyce ends *Finnegans Wake* with a structure word, pure and simple. Although it is commonly supposed to be so, I recall no conclusive evidence that the last word of the book connects with the first to form a complete circle. But even if it does, the last "the" stands alone at the end of the work, completely devoid of semantic meaning, and followed only by the remaining blank paper of the page. For "the," although it means nothing in itself, means something in relation to other words. Its sole purpose is to anticipate the next word, to guarantee that something will follow, something definite and particular. The "the" at the end of *Finnegans Wake* anticipates nothing—a definite nothing, the void, the silence, the death of ALP.

The problems of deconstruction in *Finnegans Wake* are not without implications for critics and criticism of the work. A commentator on *Finnegans Wake* ignores at her or his peril the fact that the book is itself about the quest for truth, the "true" facts, the correct interpretation, the "authentic" version, and that it purposefully levels all such pretensions. The results of critical efforts are not important in the *Wake,* but rather the compulsions and motives of the questors, their styles and methods, their quarrels, their self-justifications, and their own implication in the object of their study. Hermeneutics is an important issue in *Finnegans Wake.* It is possible, therefore, that just as Joyce provided for diverse interpretations of the hen's Letter or ALP's "mamafesto" in I.7 of the *Wake* itself, so he provided for diverse interpretations of *Finnegans Wake*. *Our Exagmination Round His Facti-fication for Incamination of Work in Progress* is a veritable extension of *Work in Progress*. While Joyce merely supervised the work of the "twelve Marshals"[34] and allowed them to write serious critical essays, he collected these into a volume that belongs nicely to the *Wake*. Besides the Wakean title, which Joyce invented and to which there is reference in the work itself (284.20), the number of essays corresponds to the number of customers and judges in the *Wake,* to the twelve apostles, twelve jurors, and so on. *Our Exagmination* was designated with a symbol (○), a designation not unlike those belonging to the *Wake* (□) and the members of the Earwicker "doodles" family: HCE (m), ALP (△), Mamalujo (X) (see 299, F4). Another projected book of four essays, to correspond to the four annalists, historians, teachers, and evangelists in the work was designated as X, but was never produced. Joyce included two letters of protest in *Our Exagmination,* one of them the priceless contribution of Vladimir Dixon, which, of course, was Joyce's own. Nothing could be more Wakean than this self-reflexive act of writing a letter to oneself about oneself.

By writing *Finnegans Wake* as he did, Joyce confirmed the impossibility of metalanguage, that is, the impossibility of making a critique in language of the epistemology embedded in language. This problem applies also to commentary *on* the *Wake*. It is difficult to write or talk about *Finnegans Wake* in conventional language. Wakean titles of critical studies, *Eternal Geomater* and *Joyce-Again's Wake,* for example, and often the text itself—"The hen's 'culdee sacco of wabbash' (210.1) does not sound too hopeful, nor does the prospect of 'potluck' for her children 'for evil and ever' " (210.5–6), writes Tindall[35] —confirm the dependence of the critic on *Wake* language. Perhaps *Wake* critics and their interpretations form merely one dimension in the infinite regress that characterizes the hermeneutic theme of *Finnegans Wake*. Perhaps like the *Wake* citizenry itself, we investigate the sin in Phoenix Park, wondering what happened, trying to identify the principals, quarreling among ourselves, coming up with conflicting and contradictory versions, engaged in a love/hate relationship with the father, Joyce, and all the while examining insomniacally the seemingly unintelligible Letter under lamplight, muttering softly, "Bethicket me for a stump of a beech if I have the poultriest notions what the farest he all means" (112.5).

NOTES

INTRODUCTION

1. Samuel Beckett et al., *Our Exagmination Round His Factification for Incamination of Work in Progress* (New York: New Directions Books, 1962).

2. Michael H. Begnal and Fritz Senn, eds., *A Conceptual Guide to "Finnegans Wake"* (University Park: Pennsylvania State University Press, 1974), p. x.

3. Eugene Jolas, "My Friend James Joyce," in Seon Givens, ed., *James Joyce: Two Decades of Criticism* (New York: Vanguard Press, 1963), p. 11.

4. Eugene Jolas, "The Revolution of Language and James Joyce," in Beckett et al., p. 79.

5. Ibid., pp. 84–85.

6. The available evidence indicates that Joyce attended a lecture on experimental linguistics by Père Marcel Jousse in 1931, although its effect on *Finnegans Wake* is uncertain. See Richard Ellmann, *James Joyce* (New York: Oxford University Press, 1965), p. 647. Joyce's personal library contained virtually no works on linguistic theory per se. Thomas Connolly in *The Personal Library of James Joyce,* does list H. L. Mencken's *The American Language* and texts on auxiliary languages, Charles Kay Ogden's *Basic English* and *Debabelization,* "with a Survey of Contemporary Opinion on the Problem of Universal Language." Other language books in the personal library include foreign language dictionaries and dictionaries of slang, as well as texts on usage and etiquette: Basil Hargrave's *Origins and Meanings of Popular Phrases and Names Including Those Which Came into Use during the Great War,* also *English as She Is Spoke: Or a Jest in Sober Earnest,* and Ogden's *Brighter Basic: Examples of Basic English for Young Persons of Taste and Feeling.* See Thomas E. Connolly, *The Personal Library of James Joyce: A Descriptive Bibliography* (Buffalo: The University of Buffalo Bookstore, 1957); Ronald Buckalew, "Night Lessons on Language," in Begnal and Senn, pp. 93–115, also contains a helpful discussion of Joyce's linguistic background.

7. Jacques Lacan, "The Function of Language in Psychoanalysis," in Anthony Wilden, *The Language of the Self* (Baltimore: The Johns Hopkins University Press, 1968).

8. James Joyce, *Letters of James Joyce,* ed. Stuart Gilbert (New York: Viking Press, 1966), 1:226. From a letter to Harriet Shaw Weaver dated 27 January 1925.

9. Frederic Jameson, "Metacommentary," *PMLA* 86, no. 1 (January 1971):14.

10. Frederick J. Hoffman, "Infroyce," in Givens, pp. 390–435.

11. James S. Atherton, *The Books at the Wake* (New York: Viking Press, 1960), pp. 37–39.

12. Clive Hart, *Structure and Motif in "Finnegans Wake"* (London: Faber and Faber, 1962), Chapter 3.

13. Sigmund Freud, "The Interpretation of Dreams," in *The Standard Edition of the Complete Psychological Works of Sigmund Freud,* trans. James Strachey (London: The Hogarth Press, 1953–74), 4:241–76.

14. Ibid., p. 201.

CHAPTER ONE

1. Harry Levin, review in *New Directions* (1939), in Robert Deming, ed., *James Joyce: The Critical Heritage,* 2 vols. (New York: Barnes & Noble, 1970), 2: 695–96.

2. Adaline Glasheen, *A Second Census of "Finnegans Wake"* (Evanston, Ill.: Northwestern University Press, 1963), pp. 38–41.

3. Herman Melville, "Billy Budd," in *Great Short Works of Herman Melville* (New York: Harper and Row, 1966), p. 358.

4. Clive Hart, *Structure and Motif in "Finnegans Wake"* (London: Faber and Faber, 1962), pp. 83–93.

5. James S. Atherton, *The Books at the Wake* (New York: Viking Press, 1960), p. 13.

6. Michael H. Begnal and Fritz Senn, eds., *A Conceptual Guide to "Finnegans Wake"* (University Park: Pennsylvania State University Press, 1974), pp. 174–75.

7. Ibid., p. 178.

8. Ibid., p. 174.

9. See William York Tindall, *A Reader's Guide to "Finnegans Wake"* (New York: Farrar, Straus and Giroux, 1969), Chapter 14.

10. The references to Boucicault's "Shaun the Post," cited by Atherton, pp. 157–61, occur in these first three chapters of Book III.

11. Tindall, pp. 237–39.

12. Ibid., p. 250.

CHAPTER TWO

1. William York Tindall, *A Reader's Guide to "Finnegans Wake"* (New York: Farrar, Straus and Giroux, 1969), p. 98.

2. Clive Hart, *Structure and Motif in "Finnegans Wake"* (London: Faber and Faber, 1962), pp. 84–93.

3. Samuel Beckett et al., *Our Exagmination Round His Factification for Incamination of Work in Progress* (New York: New Directions Books, 1962), pp. 4–12.

4. Claude Lévi-Strauss, *The Savage Mind* (Chicago: University of Chicago Press, 1969), p. 234.

5. Marcel Brion, "The Ideal of Time in the Work of James Joyce," in Beckett et al., p. 32.

6. Ibid.

7. Claude Lévi-Strauss, *Structural Anthropology,* trans. Claire Jacobson and Brooke Grundfest Schoepf (New York: Doubleday, 1967), p. 198.

8. Ibid., p. 198.

9. Richard Ellmann, *James Joyce* (New York: Oxford University Press, 1965), p. 557.

10. Tindall, p. 47.

11. Ibid., p. 5.

12. Lévi-Strauss, *Structural Anthropology,* p. 226.

13. Ibid., pp. 202–28.

14. Tindall, p. 10.

15. James S. Atherton, *The Books at the Wake* (New York: Viking Press, 1960), p. 32.

16. Bernard Benstock, *Joyce-Again's Wake* (Seattle: University of Washington Press, 1965), pp. 268–96.

17. *The Frog King and Other Tales of the Brothers Grimm,* trans. Alfred and Mary Elizabeth Davis (New York: New American Library, 1964), pp. 29–35.

CHAPTER THREE

1. See Genesis 2: 19–20 for Adam's naming of the animals at God's behest.

2. Anthony Wilden, "Lacan and the Discourse of the Other," *The Language of the Self* (Baltimore: The Johns Hopkins University Press, 1968), p. 177. Wilden, referring to a native in a theoretically "authentic" primitive society, remarks, "In other words, in the ideal case, he cannot pose the question of identity, because he has already been identified (as the mother's brother, for example). The question of identity may be for him a meaningless and therefore unaskable question. . . . "

3. Claude Lévi-Strauss, *Structural Anthropology,* trans. Claire Jacobson and Brooke Grundfest Schoepf (New York: Doubleday, 1967), p. 59.

4. Joseph Campbell and Henry Morton Robinson, *A Skeleton Key to "Finnegans Wake"* (New York: Viking Press, 1969), p. 217.

5. The primal scene is the phenomenon of the child watching his parents copulate. In the famous "Wolf Man" case, Freud reports the primal scene expressed in a dream by reversal: instead of watching the kinetic scene, the frozen wolves watch the child. See "The Dream and the Primal Scene," in Sigmund Freud, "History of an Infantile Neurosis," in *The Standard Edition of the Complete Psychological Works of Sigmund Freud* (London: The Hogarth Press, 1953–74), 17: 29–47.

6. Norman O. Brown, *Love's Body* (New York: Random House, 1966), p. 54.

7. Helmut Bonheim, *Joyce's Benefictions* (Los Angeles: University of California Press, 1964), p. 47.

8. Brown, p. 5.

9. James S. Atherton, *The Books at the Wake* (New York: Viking Press, 1960), p. 53.

10. René Girard, *Deceit, Desire, and the Novel,* trans. Yvonne Freccero (Baltimore: The Johns Hopkins University Press, 1969), p. 7. For Freud's treatment of this theme, see Sigmund Freud, "Contributions to the Psychology of Love: A Special Type of Choice of Object Made by Men," *Collected Papers,* trans. Joan Riviere (London: The Hogarth Press, 1950), 4: 192–202.

11. Alexandre Kojève, *Introduction to the Reading of Hegel,* ed. Allan Bloom, trans. James H. Nichols, Jr. (New York: Basic Books, 1969), p. 7.

12. Brown, p. 6. Vico writes much the same thing, "Among the ancient Romans the family fathers had a sovereign power of life and death over their children and a despotic dominion over the property they acquired, so that down to imperial times there was no difference between sons and slaves as holders of property." Giambattista Vico, *The New Science of Giambattista Vico,* trans. Thomas Goddard Bergin and Max Harold Fisch (Ithaca: Cornell University Press, 1970), p. 153.

13. Campbell and Robinson, p. 12.

14. Wilden, pp. 160–61.

15. According to Campbell and Robinson, this segment refers to an allegorical picture of two boxers, hanging on the twins' nursery wall, and representing, of course, the twins themselves. See p. 169.

16. Wilden, p. 161.

17. The "lifewand" of Mercius is probably derived from Vico's discussion of the rod of

Mercury. "From this underworld Mercury with his rod bearing the agrarian law summons the souls from Orcus, the all-devouring monster. . . . The rod was later used by the mages in the vain belief that it had power to bring back the dead." Vico, *The New Science,* p. 221. Note that Shem's lifewand gives speech, or language, to the dumb.

18. Lévi-Strauss, *Structural Anthropology,* p. 193.

19. Atherton, pp. 40-41.

20. Wilden, p. 173.

21. Atherton, pp. 124–36.

22. Freud, "On Narcissism: An Introduction," *Collected Papers,* 4:46.

23. Vico, *The New Science,* p. xxvi.

24. Jacques Lacan, "The Function of Language in Psychoanalysis," in Wilden, p. 40.

25. Ibid.

26. Atherton, p. 31.

27. Lacan, p. 41.

28. Wilden, p. 271.

29. See Clive Hart, *Structure and Motif in "Finnegans Wake"* (London: Faber and Faber, 1962), p. 222, who cites over fifty occurrences of the motifs.

30. Wilden, p. 305, reports an anthropological account of family structure.

31. Atherton, p. 102.

32. Edmund L. Epstein, *The Ordeal of Stephen Dedalus* (Carbondale: Southern Illinois University Press, 1971), p. 12.

33. William York Tindall, *A Reader's Guide to "Finnegans Wake"* (New York: Farrar, Straus and Giroux, 1969), p. 18.

34. Vico, *The New Science,* p. 221.

35. Note the juxtaposition of "Lex" and "Lax," suggesting law and the nonobservance of law, in this catalogue of HCE's names.

36. Freud, "Totem and Taboo," in *The Standard Edition,* 13: 143.

37. Wilden, p. 271.

38. Adaline Glasheen, *A Second Census of "Finnegans Wake"* (Evanston, Ill.: Northwestern University Press, 1963), p. 20.

39. See Margaret C. Solomon, *Eternal Geomater* (Carbondale: Southern Illinois University Press, 1969), p. 95. "Joyce is not simply indulging his urge to include in *Finnegans Wake* every tabooed subject he can think of; for purposes of a tight symbolic pattern, he seems to stress the expression of male-to-male intercourse in sodomy (that is, anal homosexuality between two male humans). One must somehow visualize a two-sided protagonist, acting heterosexually in one direction and allowing himself to be acted upon, homosexually, behind his back."

40. Similar words, such as "lasso" and "barrel," occur in the description of Stephen's urination in "Proteus." "In long lassoes from the Cock lake the water flowed full. . . . In cups of rocks it slops: flop, slop, slap: bounded in barrels" (*U,* p. 49).

41. Atherton, p. 102.

42. Marcel Brion, "The Idea of Time in the Work of James Joyce," in Beckett et al., *Our Exagmination Round His Factification* for *Incamination of Work in Progress* (New York: New Directions Books, 1962), p. 29.

43. Ibid.

44. Compare with Stephen's cash register approach to salvation in *Portrait,* p. 148.

45. Lacan, p. 35.

46. Martin Heidegger, *An Introduction to Metaphysics,* trans. Ralph Manheim (Garden City: Doubleday, 1961), p. 104.

47. Beckett, et al., p. 11.

48. Freud, "Totem and Taboo," in *The Standard Edition,* 13: 149.

49. Atherton, p. 63.

50. Tindall, p. 103.

51. Atherton, pp. 157–61.

52. Ibid., p. 158.

CHAPTER FOUR

1. William York Tindall, *A Reader's Guide to "Finnegans Wake"* (New York: Farrar, Straus and Giroux, 1969), p. 67.

2. Dounia Bunis Christiani, *Scandinavian Elements of "Finnegans Wake"* (Evanston, Ill.: Northwestern University Press, 1965), p. 99.

3. René Girard, "Lévi-Strauss, Frye, Derrida and Shakespearean Criticism," *Diacritics* 3, no. 3 (Fall 1973): 36.

4. The dream begins, "My friend R. was my uncle. . . . " See Sigmund Freud, "The Interpretation of Dreams," in *The Standard Edition of the Complete Psychological Works of Sigmund Freud,* trans. James Strachey (London: The Hogarth Press, 1953–74), 4: 137.

5. Robert Boyle discusses the artistic process of this chapter in terms of magic artifacts in Wilde and Balzac. See "The Artist as Balzacian Wilde Ass," in Michael H. Begnal and Fritz Senn, eds., *A Conceptual Guide to "Finnegans Wake"* (University Park: Pennsylvania State University Press, 1974), pp. 71–82.

6. Jacques Lacan, "The Function of Language in Psychoanalysis," in Anthony Wilden, *The Language of the Self* (Baltimore: The Johns Hopkins University Press, 1968), p. 21.

7. Martin Heidegger, *Being and Time,* trans. John Macquairie and Edward Robinson (New York: Harper and Row, 1962), p. 208.

8. Philip L. Graham discovered an extensive scapegoat motif in the recurrent image of the pig in this chapter. See "The Middlewhite Fair," in *A Wake Newslitter* 6, no. 5 (October 1969): 67–69. While Graham maintains that Hyacinth is the name of the pedigreed pig in the section, he does not explicitly say that the pig/scapegoat may be a persecuted homosexual, perhaps Lord Alfred Douglas whom Wilde called "Hyacinthus" after the beautiful youth loved by the gods. "Roaring O'Crian, Jr." may refer to William O'Brien, founder of the United Irish League, who exposed homosexuals in the police department and post office, according to Adaline Glasheen in *A Second Census of "Finnegans Wake,"* (Evanston, Ill.: Northwestern University Press, 1963), p. 189. References to the Parnell Commission via John MacDonald (Hyacinth O'Donnell) add political martyrs to the scapegoat motif (William O'Brien was once jailed with Parnell). Another political scapegoat referred to in "Roaring O'Crian, Jr." may be William Smith O'Brien, the rival of Daniel O'Connell, who, like HCE, was tried, condemned to death, exiled, and finally pardoned—"Left the tribunal scotfree" (93.3). O'Connell and William O'Brien both promoted reform of the rent system—O'Brien wrote the "No Rent Manifesto"— and are therefore connected to the theme of failure to pay the rent in this chapter. Besides persecuted homosexuals and politicians, the passage contains reference to two religious figures, William O'Bryan, who founded the Bible Christian Church, an offshoot of Wesleyan Method-ism—"whom Wesleyan chapelgoers suspected of being a plain clothes priest" (86.33)—and Charles Loyson, known as "Père Hyacinthe," who founded the Gallican Church in Paris.

9. Heidegger, *Being and Time,* p. 212.

10. Hugh Kenner, *Dublin's Joyce* (London: Chatto and Windus, 1955), p. 7.

11. Ibid.

12. Lacan, p. 15.

13. Heidegger, *Being and Time,* p. 334.

14. James S. Atherton, *The Books at the Wake* (New York: Viking Press, 1960), p. 98.

15. Ibid.

16. James Joyce, *Letters of James Joyce,* ed. Stuart Gilbert (New York: Viking Press, 1966), 1: 406. Letter to Frank Budgen dated 20 August 1939.

17. See Bernard Benstock, *Joyce-Again's Wake* (Seattle: University of Washington Press, 1965), p. 97.

18. Martin Heidegger, "On the Essence of Truth," trans. R. F. C. Hull and Alan Crick, in *Existence and Being* (Chicago: Henry Regnery Company, 1968), p. 309.

19. Ibid., p. 303.

20. Although he doesn't stress the connection, Robert Boyle's discussion of Matthew Arnold and Joyce clearly has a bearing on the archdruid-Berkeley debate. See "The Artist as Balzacian Wilde Ass," in *Begnal and Senn,* p. 72.

21. Heidegger, *Being and Time,* p. 265.

22. Benstock, p. 103.

23. Wilden, p. 166.

24. Stuart Schneiderman, "Afloat with Jacques Lacan," *Diacritics* 1, no. 2 (Winter 1971): 29.

25. Heidegger, *Being and Time,* p. 297.

26. Richard Ellmann, *James Joyce* (New York: Oxford University Press, 1965), p. 557.

27. Ibid., p. 138.

28. Leo Tolstoy, *The Death of Ivan Ilych and Other Stories* (New York: The New American Library, 1960), p. 101.

29. Heidegger, *Being and Time,* p. 294.

30. Tolstoy, p. 147.

31. Heidegger, *Being and Time,* p. 310.

CHAPTER FIVE

1. Edmund Wilson, *Axel's Castle* (New York: Charles Scribner's Sons, 1969), pp. 234–35.

2. Clive Hart, *Structure and Motif in "Finnegans Wake"* (London: Faber and Faber, 1962), p. 31.

3. Wilson, p. 228.

4. Hart, p. 82.

5. Ibid., p. 93.

6. Hart claims that Joyce hated psychoanalysis and "used only so much of its techniques and *Weltanschauung* as he found useful," p. 82. Hart consequently looks to the Upanishads for the dream theory underlying *Finnegans Wake.* "The several appearances of the words OM, AUM, in *Finnegans Wake,* and the thematic use of the important 'Silence,' make it seem highly likely that Joyce moulded his succession of dream-levels very largely on the AUM states," p. 99. See Frederick J. Hoffman, in Seon Givens, ed., *James Joyce: Two Decades of Criticism* (New York: Vanguard Press, 1963), pp. 390–435, and James S. Atherton, *The Books at the Wake* (New York: Viking Press, 1960), pp. 37–39, for evidence in support of Joyce's knowledge and use of the works of Freud. Also, see Leonard Albert, *Joyce and the New Psychology,* Ph.D. diss., Columbia University (Ann Arbor, Mich.: University Microfilms, 1957).

7. Sigmund Freud, "The Interpretation of Dreams," in *The Standard Edition of the Complete Psychological Works of Sigmund Freud,* trans. James Strachey (London: The Hogarth Press, 1953–74), 4: 107 details the dream of Irma's injection; ibid., p. 296 gives reference to "norekdal;" and ibid., p. 232 gives reference to "gen Italien." Also see "Espe," in "History of an Infantile Neurosis," in *The Standard Edition,* 17: 94.

8. Freud, "The Interpretation of Dreams," in *The Standard Edition,* 4: 277–78.

9. James Joyce, *Letters of James Joyce,* ed. Richard Ellmann (New York: Viking Press, 1966), 3: 146. From a letter to Harriet Shaw Weaver dated 24 November 1926.

10. Jacques Lacan, "The Insistence of the Letter in the Unconscious," trans. Jan Miel in *Structuralism,* ed. Jacques Ehrmann (New York: Doubleday, 1970), pp. 101–37.

11. Freud, *The Standard Edition,* 6.

12. Freud, "The Interpretation of Dreams," in *The Standard Edition,* 4: 452.

13. Atherton, p. 96; and William York Tindall, *A Reader's Guide to "Finnegans Wake"* (New York: Farrar, Straus and Giroux, 1969), p. 117.

14. Lacan, *Structuralism,* p. 119.

15. Freud cites a joke that involves a curiously similar punning between silver and trees. "What is the cheapest way of obtaining silver? You go down an avenue of silver poplars and call for silence. The babbling then ceases and the silver is released." "The Interpretation of Dreams," in *The Standard Edition,* 4: 297. Joyce also uses the conjunction of "sylvia" and "silence" twice, in 61.1 and 337.16.

16. Tindall, p. 5.

17. Sigmund Freud, "Notes Upon a Case of Obsessional Neurosis," in *Collected Papers,* trans. Alix and James Strachey (New York: Basic Books, 1959), 3: 350.

18. Lacan, *Structuralism,* p. 117.

19. Freud, "The Interpretation of Dreams," in *The Standard Edition,* 4:293.

20. Ibid., p. 104.

21. Richard Ellmann, *James Joyce* (New York: Oxford University Press, 1965), p. 626.

22. Freud, "Jokes and their Relation to the Unconscious," in *The Standard Edition,* 13:167.

23. Sigmund Freud, *A General Introduction to Psychoanalysis,* trans. Joan Riviere (New York: Washington Square Press, 1968), p. 35.

24. Joseph Campbell and Henry Morton Robinson, *A Skeleton Key to "Finnegans Wake"* (New York: Viking Press, 1969), p. 157.

25. Ibid., p. 187.

26. Lewis Carroll, "Alice in Wonderland," in *The Annotated Alice,* ed. Martin Gardner (Cleveland: The World Publishing Company, 1963), p. 129.

27. Tindall, p. 13.

CHAPTER SIX

1. Samuel Beckett et al., *Our Exagmination Round His Factification for Incamination of Work in Progress* (New York: New Directions Books, 1962), p. 14.

2. Ibid., p. 22.

3. Jacques Derrida, "Structure, Sign, and Play in the Discourse of the Human Sciences," in Richard Macksey and Eugenio Donato, eds., *The Languages of Criticism and the Sciences of Man: The Structuralist Controversy* (Baltimore: The Johns Hopkins University Press, 1970), p. 249.

4. T. E. Hulme, *Speculations,* ed. Herbert Read (New York: Harcourt, Brace and Company, 1924), p. 117.

5. Derrida, p. 249–50.

6. Ibid., p. 252.

7. William Carlos Williams, *Imaginations,* ed. Webster Schott (New York: New Directions Books, 1970), p. 93.

8. Derrida, p. 260.

9. William York Tindall, *A Reader's Guide to "Finnegans Wake"* (New York: Farrar, Straus and Giroux, 1969), p. 15.

10. Lacan, "The Function of Language in Psychoanalysis," in Anthony Wilden, *The Language of the Self* (Baltimore: The Johns Hopkins University Press, 1968), p. 40.

11. Hugh Kenner, *Dublin's Joyce* (Boston: Beacon Press, 1956), p. 304.

12. Clive Hart, *Structure and Motif in "Finnegans Wake"* (London: Faber and Faber, 1962), p. 36.

13. John Lyons, *Introduction to Theoretical Linguistics* (New York: Cambridge University Press, 1968), p. 88.

14. Ibid., p. 120.

15. Lewis Carroll, "Alice in Wonderland," in *The Annotated Alice,* ed. Martin Gardner (Cleveland: The World Publishing Company, 1963), p. 197.

16. Ronald Buckalew, "Night Lessons on Language," in Michael H. Begnal and Fritz Senn, eds., *A Conceptual Guide to "Finnegans Wake"* (University Park: Pennsylvania State University Press, 1974), p. 105.

17. James Joyce, *Letters of James Joyce,* ed. Stuart Gilbert (New York: Viking Press, 1966), 1: 237. From a letter to Harriet Shaw Weaver dated 11 November 1925.

18. Richard Ellmann, *James Joyce* (New York: Oxford University Press, 1965), p. 558.

19. Hart, p. 44.

20. Ibid., p. 35.

21. Joyce, *Letters,* 1: 194. From a letter to Mrs. William Murray dated 10 November 1922.

22. Claude Lévi-Strauss, *The Savage Mind* (Chicago: University of Chicago Press, 1969), p. 18.

23. David Hayman describes how Joyce wrote the draft for the introduction of II.2, working directly from the notes in his workbook. "Of the 266 words in the completed first draft approximately 132 can be traced directly to the notes." See "Scribbledehobbles' and How they Grew: A Turning Point in the Development of a Chapter," in Jack P. Dalton and Clive Hart, eds., *Twelve and a Tilly* (Evanston, Ill.: Northwestern University Press, 1965), p. 110.

24. Lévi-Strauss, *The Savage Mind,* p. 21.

25. Ellmann, p. 50.

26. Ibid., p. 51.

27. Ibid., p. 594.

28. Hart, pp. 53–55.

29. Ellmann, p. 558.

30. Joyce, *Letters,* 1: 204. Letter to Harriet Shaw Weaver dated 9 October 1923.

31. Lévi-Strauss, *The Savage Mind,* p. 21.

32. Joyce, *Letters,* 1: 204.

33. William Carlos Williams, from "William Carlos Williams on Joyce's Style," in Robert Deming, ed., *James Joyce: The Critical Heritage,* 2 vols. (New York: Barnes & Noble, 1970), 1: 377.

34. Ellmann, p. 626.

35. Tindall, p. 145.

BIBLIOGRAPHY

I. WORKS RELATED TO JOYCE AND *FINNEGANS WAKE:*

Atherton, James S. *The Books at the Wake.* New York: Viking Press, 1960.

Beckett, Samuel, et al. *Our Exagmination Round His Factification for Incamination of Work in Progress.* New York: New Directions Books, 1962.

Begnal, Michael H. "Who Speaks When I Dream? Who Dreams When I Speak?: A Narrational Approach to *Finnegans Wake.*" The University of Tulsa Monograph Series 13 (1971): 74–90.

Begnal, Michael H., and Senn, Fritz, eds. *A Conceptual Guide to "Finnegans Wake."* University Park: Pennsylvania State University Press, 1974.

Benstock, Bernard. *Joyce-Again's Wake.* Seattle: University of Washington Press, 1965.

Bonheim, Helmut. *Joyce's Benefictions.* Berkeley: University of California Press, 1964.

Budgen, Frank. *Myselves When Young.* New York: Oxford University Press, 1970.

Campbell, Joseph, and Robinson, Henry Morton. *A Skeleton Key to "Finnegans Wake."* New York: Viking Press, 1969.

Christiani, Dounia Bunis. *Scandinavian Elements of "Finnegans Wake."* Evanston, Ill.: Northwestern University Press, 1965.

Connolly, Thomas E. *The Personal Library of James Joyce: A Descriptive Bibliography.* Buffalo: The University of Buffalo Bookstore, 1957.

Dalton, Jack P., and Hart, Clive, eds. *Twelve and a Tilly.* Evanston, Ill.: Northwestern University Press, 1965.

Deming, Robert, ed. *James Joyce: The Critical Heritage.* 2 vols. New York: Barnes & Noble, 1970.

Ellmann, Richard. *James Joyce.* New York: Oxford University Press, 1965.

Epstein, Edmund. *The Ordeal of Stephen Dedalus.* Carbondale: Southern Illinois University Press, 1971.

Givens, Seon, ed. *James Joyce: Two Decades of Criticism.* New York: Vanguard Press, 1963.

Glasheen, Adaline. *A Second Census of "Finnegans Wake."* Evanston, Ill.: Northwestern University Press, 1963.

Graham, Philip L. "The Middlewhite Fair." *A Wake Newslitter* 6 (October 1969): 67–69.

Hart, Clive. *Structure and Motif in "Finnegans Wake."* Evanston, Ill.: Northwestern University Press, 1962.

Joyce, James. *Letters of James Joyce.* Vol. 1, edited by Stuart Gilbert. New York: Viking Press, 1966.

———. *Letters of James Joyce.* Vol. 3, edited by Richard Ellmann. New York: Viking Press, 1966.

Kenner, Hugh. *Dublin's Joyce.* Boston: Beacon Press, 1956.

Litz, A. Walton. *The Art of James Joyce.* New York: Oxford University Press, 1968.

O Hehir, Brendan. *A Gaelic Lexicon for "Finnegans Wake."* Berkeley: University of California Press, 1967.

Solomon, Margaret. *Eternal Geomater.* Carbondale: Southern Illinois University Press, 1969.

Tindall, William York. *A Reader's Guide to "Finnegans Wake."* New York: Farrar, Straus and Giroux, 1969.

Vico, Giambattista. *The New Science of Giambattista Vico.* Translated by Thomas Bergin and Max Fisch. Ithaca: Cornell University Press, 1970.

Wilson, Edmund. *Axel's Castle.* New York: Charles Scribner's Sons, 1969.

II. WORKS RELATED TO STRUCTURALIST THEORY:

Barthes, Roland. *Elements of Semiology.* Translated by Annette Lavers and Colin Smith. New York: Hill & Wang, 1968.

Brown, Norman O. *Love's Body.* New York: Vintage Books, 1966.

Ehrmann, Jacques, ed. *Structuralism.* New York: Doubleday, 1970.

Freud, Sigmund. *Collected Papers.* Vol. 3, translated by Alix and James Strachey. Vol. 4, translated by Joan Riviere. 5 vols. New York: Basic Books, 1959.

———. *A General Introduction to Psychoanalysis.* Translated by Joan Riviere. New York: Washington Square Press, 1968.

———. *The Standard Edition of the Complete Psychological Works of Sigmund Freud.* Translated by James Strachey. 24 vols. London: The Hogarth Press, 1953–74.

Girard, René. *Deceit, Desire, and the Novel.* Translated by Yvonne Freccero. Baltimore: The Johns Hopkins University Press, 1969.

———. "Lévi-Strauss, Frye, Derrida and Shakespearean Criticism." *Diacritics* 3 (Fall 1973): 34–38.

Heidegger, Martin. *Being and Time.* Translated by John Macquarrie and Edward Robinson. New York: Harper and Row, 1962.

———. *Existence and Being.* Chicago: Henry Regnery Co., 1968.

———. *An Introduction to Metaphysics.* Translated by Ralph Manheim. New York: Doubleday, 1961.

Hulme, T. E. *Speculations.* Edited by Herbert Read. New York: Doubleday, 1961.

Jameson, Frederic. "Metacommentary." *PMLA* 86 (January 1971): 9–17.

Kojève, Alexandre. *Introduction to the Reading of Hegel.* Edited by Allan Bloom. Translated by James H. Nichols, Jr. New York: Basic Books, 1969.

Lévi-Strauss, Claude. *The Savage Mind.* Chicago: University of Chicago Press, 1969.

——. *Structural Anthropology.* Translated by Claire Jacobson and Brooke Grundfest Schoepf. New York: Doubleday, 1967.

Lyons, John. *Introduction to Theoretical Linguistics.* New York: Cambridge University Press, 1968.

Macksey, Richard, and Donato, Eugenio, eds. *The Languages of Criticism and the Sciences of Man: The Structuralist Controversy.* Baltimore: The Johns Hopkins University Press, 1970.

Schneiderman, Stuart. "Afloat with Jacques Lacan." *Diacritics* 1 (Winter 1971): 27–34.

Wilden, Anthony. *The Language of the Self.* Baltimore: The Johns Hopkins University Press, 1968.

The Johns Hopkins University Press

*This book was composed in Aldine Roman text and
Windsor Light Condensed Display type by The Composing Room
from a design by Marlene Bressler. It was printed on 50-lb.
Publishers Eggshell Wove paper and bound in Holliston Roxite A
vellum cloth by The Maple Press Company.*

Library of Congress Cataloging in Publication Data

Norris, Margot.
   The decentered universe of *Finnegans Wake*.

   Bibliography: p. 149
   1. Joyce, James, 1882–1941. Finnegans wake.
2. Dreams in literature. I. Title.
PR6019.09F59364   823'.9'12   76–25507
ISBN 0–8018–1820–6